CAMBRIDGE International Exam

Professional Development for Teachers

Teaching and Assessing Skills in
First Language English

Tony Parkinson

CAMBRIDGE
UNIVERSITY PRESS

PUBLISHED BY THE PRESS SYNDICATE OF THE UNIVERSITY OF CAMBRIDGE
The Pitt Building, Trumpington Street, Cambridge, United Kingdom

CAMBRIDGE UNIVERSITY PRESS
The Edinburgh Building, Cambridge CB2 2RU, UK
40 West 20th Street, New York, NY 10011-4211, USA
477 Williamstown Road, Port Melbourne, VIC 3207, Australia
Ruiz de Alarcón 13, 28014 Madrid, Spain
Dock House, The Waterfront, Cape Town 8001, South Africa

http://www.cambridge.org

© Cambridge International Examinations 2002

First published 2002

Printed in the United Kingdom at the University Press, Cambridge

Typefaces Dax, Meridien, Officina   *System* QuarkXPress®

A catalogue record for this book is available from the British Library

ISBN 0 521 75355 4 paperback

The publisher has used its best endeavours to ensure that the URLs
for external websites referred to in this book are correct and active
at the time of going to press. However, the publisher has no
responsibility for the websites and can make no guarantee that a
site will remain live or that the content will remain appropriate.

Contents

Foreword

Teaching is a complex and demanding profession. All over the world, societies change in response to new knowledge gained, technological developments, globalisation and a requirement for an ever-more sophisticated and educated population. Teachers are in the forefront of such social change, responding with speed and confidence to the new demands made of them, in terms of both their knowledge and the way in which they teach. This series is intended to help them in their adaptation to change and in their professional development as teachers.

Curriculum changes worldwide are putting increased emphasis on the acquisition of skills as well as subject knowledge, so that students will have the ability to respond flexibly to the swiftly changing modern environment. As a result, teachers must be able both to teach and assess skills and to adjust their own teaching methods to embrace a wider range of techniques for both teaching and assessing in the classroom. The books in this series are practical handbooks which explore these techniques and offer advice on how to use them to enhance the teacher's own practice.

The handbooks are written by teachers with direct experience of teaching and assessing skills at this level. We have asked them to write for their readers in such a way that the readers feel directly supported in their professional development. Thus, as well as tasks for students, there are tasks for teachers, pauses for reflection and questions to be answered. We hope that readers will find that this mixture of the practical and the professional helps them, both in their practice and in their own sense of what it means to be an effective teacher in this modern, changing world of international education.

Dr Kate Pretty
Series Editor

Introduction

The purpose and contents of this book

Teaching English as a first language is a pleasure and a privilege, but there is so much to cover. Teachers often ask for advice in presenting a coherent English curriculum to their students. This book offers coherence by concentrating on communicative skills, in particular:

- suggesting ways of developing the wide range of skills that all students need in order to make progress;
- showing how these skills are interrelated;
- demonstrating how they can be translated into classroom practice and suggesting where it would be helpful to set up departmental policies;
- highlighting opportunities to discuss and work out ideas with colleagues.

The main part of the book has been divided into speaking and listening, reading, and writing. In the chapter on speaking and listening, the emphasis is on these skills as a means to an end, and examples are given of speaking and listening activities that also involve reading and writing and that are a gateway to thinking logically and creatively for oneself.

The chapter on reading shows how to support students in improving both their skills and their interests, and suggests ways in which they can use and share their reading experiences.

The chapter on writing considers approaches to different types of writing and discusses style and register. It also includes approaches to technical aspects of writing.

The next chapter is about some issues peculiar to coursework, that is the collecting together of students' best work over a period of time as an alternative to terminal examinations. Lastly, there is an approach to assessment in the classroom.

The book concentrates mainly on teaching fifteen- to sixteen-year-olds, but, where necessary, also includes earlier steps in skill teaching. In any case, the acquisition of skills is common to all age groups and abilities.

The book does not refer to any particular examination and is meant to apply to the advancement of students' educational standards, however these may be assessed.

Teaching styles

With such a wealth of curricular content, it is hard to find two teachers whose attitudes towards what and how to teach coincide. Perhaps you belong to a liberal, creative tradition, or you may be a hard-line grammarian. Your school may even require you to be one or the other. You may believe in a brief introduction to a lesson followed by busy student interaction, or you may prefer to teach and test while your students learn by listening.

This book tends to take the middle way and it only suggests ways forward. Your reaction may be, 'Oh, I wouldn't do that,' but your mind might move on to say, 'It gives me ideas for something that could be really worthwhile.' If it promotes that sort of positive discussion, then the book will have had some success.

What 'First Language English' means

The term first-language English refers to a standard of linguistic proficiency which determines a certain teaching style and which allows for the exploration of a wide range of issues, texts and media experiences of a challenging nature.

For many first-language standard students, English is their family language, while other students are truly bilingual, or may attend schools where some lessons are conducted in, say, Spanish or Arabic, and the rest in English. Others attend international schools where the language of instruction is English and where so many nationalities are represented that English also becomes the language of leisure. Many are multilingual, but their command of English is equivalent to that of a first-language user. Finally, there are countries whose language is relatively unknown abroad or who for economic or political reasons insist that all their students learn English.

All these students will have progressed beyond the first stages of learning English and will be able to use it with competence and fluency in a variety of situations. Their style of speaking or writing will often be peculiar to a particular sort of teaching or to a geographical location, but this diversity will be readily acceptable to other users.

Skills for life outside the classroom

Students often ask the question, 'Why are we doing this?', so as a first step in using this book, we could consider their reasons for needing English in the workplace, at home and when travelling.

Teacher activity (discussion)

Look at each of the following in turn. What skills would students need to carry out each successfully, and how would you teach them? Keep a list of the skills you have mentioned.

In the workplace
- Talk to clients on the telephone. Take part in videoconferences with people in other countries. Meet clients who only speak English.
- Read and answer correspondence. Respond to emails.
- Read, summarise, use and respond to documents in magazines and on the Internet that may be useful in the development of ideas and the running of the company.
- (In tourism) meet and respond to the needs of tourists who do not know the local language. Act as interpreter.

At home
- Read to children. Monitor their language (either first language or bilingual).
- Read and write (poetry, stories, plays) for their own pleasure and for the entertainment of others.
- Research on the Internet (this is a very high degree skill).

Travel
- Use English as a common language in countries you visit where you are not conversant with the language (e.g. as a tourist from the Netherlands visiting a hotel in Portugal).

So now let us move on and look at the different skills that make up First Language English.

1 Skills in First Language English

Curricular skills

The curricular skills are:
- speaking and listening;
- reading;
- writing.

Note that speaking and listening are always regarded as one in first-language work, although speaking is known as a productive skill and listening as a receptive skill. Listening is nevertheless best demonstrated by what is said in response, not by the posture adopted by the listener. At its simplest, you know that a student has listened effectively by the quality of an answer to your question or comment. Written tests of listening are not normally used in first-language work.

> ### Teacher activity 1.1 (planning)
>
> Plan a lesson, based on a topic you are currently teaching, which includes some reading, some speaking and listening and some writing. Allot a time to each section, allowing for your brief introduction to the lesson and the conclusion. Alternatively, plan a whole week's work, showing the balance between speaking and listening, reading, writing and teacher talk.

Technical skills

These are the essentials of writing and consist of:
- spelling;
- punctuation;
- grammar (including the correct use of tense) and grammatical devices;
- paragraphing and sequencing;

- the acquisition of a wide and effective vocabulary;
- sentence structures.

Some of these skills are also applicable to speaking and listening. For example, failure to have the right words at their disposal makes students' contributions to discussion ineffective. Both writing and speaking and listening can be assessed by using fluency as a criterion. Fluency is normally a product of sentence construction and sequencing sentences in a logical order. A writer whose work is fluent will attract the reader and make comprehension easy; a speaker who is fluent assists comfortable listening. A student can also see technical skills in action through reading.

Thinking skills

Language can only function on a simple level without thinking. Indeed, there is a good case to be made for changing 'speaking and listening' to 'listening, thinking and speaking'. You would get more considered responses!

The main thinking skills are to:
- **analyse**, or take to pieces – a simple example is a summary; more complicated is an account of an experiment to discover the composition of a substance, or an explanation of the ways in which a composer develops a motif in a piece of music;
- **synthesise**, or put together – an example would be the use of several documents to make a compendium of explanations of different arguments made about the treatment of animals;
- **evaluate**, or comment and make a judgement – perhaps on two poems on the same subject, with one judged by the reader as more realistic and effective than the other;
- **create**, or realise an idea, invent, brainstorm, describe, narrate from imagination and experience.

Personal skills

These skills apply to each student's general development and progress, especially in speaking and listening. The main personal skills are:
- **confidence in themselves** – making contributions and developing them, expressing preferences and showing pride in what they do, arguing against the majority where it becomes necessary, reading to others (especially younger children) and helping others with their reading;
- **respecting others** – listening to what they say, acknowledging their opinions, adopting appropriate forms of address, enjoying each other's work;

- **managing conversation** – taking charge, following an agenda, persuading others to express opinions, not dominating;
- **taking roles** – adapting the part one plays and one's language to the situation, e.g. reporting back, debating, note-taking, reflecting, facilitating, acting.

Skills in performance

Here are two examples that show the complexity with which these skills interrelate in the classroom. Do they happen by accident or can you plan them to happen? If you plan them, you can also assess students' performances.

Student activity 1.1	interrelated skills

- Class silently reads Chapter 3 of *Picnic at Hanging Rock* (from: 'At every step the prospect ahead grew more enchanting with added detail of crenellated crags and lichen-patterned stone.')
- Direct class to examples of dialogue, how it is set out and punctuated.
- Class reads out loud, in groups of four, the words of the girls.
- Class stays in groups to discuss (a) their impressions of Miranda and the other girls and to comment on the ways in which Lindsay portrays them; and (b) what they find odd about the end of the chapter. Each group elects one person to report back to the class.
- Teacher synthesises responses and asks class to consider ways in which dialogue is used (e.g. to suggest character, period when the novel is set, etc.).
- Writing assignment 1: The four girls are looking forward to a party at their school. Write their dialogue (as a story). Check content and punctuation/layout.
- Writing assignment 2: Continue the story from page 30 after 'vulnerable in sleep', with the words, 'Miranda awoke …' Tell the next part of the story from Miranda's point of view.

In this series of activities, the students read (silently and aloud), speak and listen (in groups while some give a report) and write. They analyse, synthesise, evaluate and create. They practise personal skills in speaking to each other and to you. They learn how dialogue is presented and its punctuation.

This complex interrelation of skills can also be shown in the following diagram.

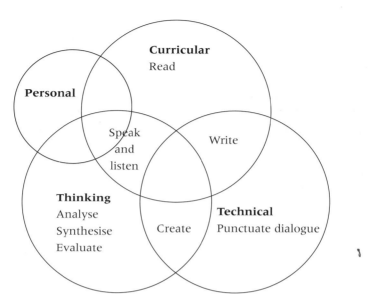

preparation for writing assignments

The class prepares in groups for continuous writing assignments based on arguments for or against controversial topics. Each group has chosen its own topic. You have provided an article from a magazine, book etc., for each group, and they have supplemented these by working in the library and on the Internet. Note that not every part of this process is suitable for groupwork and that some of it has to be done individually or in pairs. The suggested sequence of activities/events is as follows:

- Groups discuss topic and create lists of arguments for and against.
- They silently read the tabled documents (ideally individual copies).
- They make notes, either individually as they read, or as a group, discussing each document in turn.
- They discuss different ways to present the assignment, but not aiming for a consensus version.
- The first drafts are written.
- Students work in pairs to redraft writing.
- When work is complete, groups reconvene to hear students read their work.

This work not only covers all three curricular skills, but also planning, note-taking and redrafting. While reading aloud is not a part of speaking and listening, it has its place as a reading skill and in the general education and confidence building of the student.

Turning skills into objectives

Examination boards preface syllabus specifications with lists of assessment objectives. These can double usefully as learning outcomes so that, if whatever you teach fulfils the objectives at a high level, your students will have achieved well in a complete educational experience and should be able to perform well in examinations. In other words, by using the objectives, classroom practice will match examination achievement.

Before syllabus specifications for examinations are written, the objectives are decided by asking the question: 'What do you want to know about the abilities of the candidates?' When examination boards publish objectives, they establish a clear understanding between themselves and the teachers as to what is to be tested. The syllabus specification, the examination questions and the mark schemes all reflect the objectives.

In this example, the number of objectives has been kept to the minimum while covering all that needs to be assessed. Each objective is expressed as simply as possible, avoiding jargon, so it can be memorised and applied easily. Note that almost all the objectives for speaking and listening overlap with those for reading and writing – this is intentional.

Speaking and listening

Students will be assessed on their ability to:
1 listen to, understand and convey information;
2 listen to and respond appropriately to the contributions of others;
3 understand, order and present facts, ideas and opinions;
4 articulate experience and express what is thought, felt and imagined;
5 communicate clearly and fluently;
6 use language and register appropriate to audience and context.

Reading

Students will be assessed on their ability to:
1 understand information;
2 select what is relevant to specific purposes and collate information within and between texts;
3 appreciate the differences between facts, ideas and opinions;
4 recognise implicit meaning and attitudes;
5 evaluate information and detect bias;
6 appreciate a writer's use of language.

Writing

Students will be assessed on their ability to:

1 articulate experience and express what is thought, felt and imagined;
2 order and present facts, ideas and opinions;
3 use language and register appropriate to audience and context;
4 exercise control of appropriate grammatical structures;
5 understand and use a range of apt vocabulary;
6 demonstrate an awareness of the conventions of paragraphing, sentence structure, punctuation and spelling.

It is generally accepted that objectives are much easier to deal with if they are weighted evenly, that is treated with the same importance. This means that you do not get a choice as to which you should teach the most. For example, you might think that Reading objective 1 was rather boring (it is certainly not the most difficult to achieve), but students nevertheless need to practise exercises that ensure that their reading is thorough and methodical. Reading objective 4 is more attractive since you need to think more creatively and because much of the practice will come from literature, but it is probably of no more importance in the world of work than objective 1. Reading objectives 2 and 5, respectively, make specific demands on students to select and evaluate material within the contexts of particular tasks. These are in some ways the most discriminating of all the reading objectives.

These objectives bring simplicity and clarity to your planning, but in their simplicity contain a great deal of meaning. If you check them against the activities described in Student activity 1, you will find that most of the reading and speaking and listening objectives can be identified.

 LOOKING BACK

Revisit all four sets of skills that are listed here.
◆ Is there anything that you do not habitually include in a week's programme?
◆ Do you practise them without really being aware that they underpin each lesson?
◆ If you identify them in your lesson plans, does that give you chances to structure what you do more effectively?
◆ In what ways does a skill-based curriculum make it easier to plot the progress of individuals?

It is now time to see how the individual curricular skills can be developed in the classroom.

2 Speaking and listening

Why put it first? In many exams, speaking and listening is an optional extra, or carries only a relatively small weighting of the overall assessment. Yet, in the world of work, a high percentage of communication is by talk, and people are known by the way they use talk to carry out their duties with efficiency, tact or persuasion. With this in mind, perhaps we should give speaking and listening pride of place, not only as an end in itself, but – as we shall see – a way both to learn and to contribute to the planning of assignments.

The skills and purposes of speaking and listening

You will remember the list of objectives in the last chapter:
1 listen to, understand and convey information;
2 listen to and respond appropriately to the contributions of others;
3 understand, order and present facts, ideas and opinions;
4 articulate experience and express what is thought, felt and imagined;
5 communicate clearly and fluently;
6 use language and register appropriate to audience and context.

There are also skills of:
- summary;
- chairing;
- sustained explanation;
- keeping to task.

It is also a good idea to ask students to make a list of the different purposes for talk. Some of these purposes are to:

explain	describe	narrate
explore	analyse	imagine
discuss	argue	persuade

We synthesise in discussion and argument, evaluate in exploring and persuasion and create in narration and imagining.

A note on listening

The whole point of speaking and listening is that it should be interactive. Person A speaks, Person B listens, understands, considers and answers: 'This is so, isn't it ...' – 'Yes, but ...'. Perhaps we should call these skills 'Listening, thinking and speaking'. This is the process by which things get done, by which people think through a problem and find a solution.

Some listening is passive. It looks as if it is to some purpose, but the listener may be thinking, 'If I look as if I am attentive, then perhaps nobody will challenge me to speak.' It's better than looking dreamily round the room or talking to oneself, but it does not prove anything about the quality of the listening. That can only be done if the listener makes a response, such as:

- summing up previous contributions and moving the discussion on;
- answering points from a speaker;
- supporting speakers who have lost the drift of their arguments;
- revisiting what has already been said, but in other words;
- acting as note-taker and clarifying what has been written;
- asking questions after a talk and engaging the speaker in discussion.

Hence if there is no listening, there is no speaking. A student giving a talk must engage in conversation with his listeners at the end. However, questions alone may not reveal a high level of listening. The list given above includes some challenging listening and speaking skills. It follows that reading aloud may not be counted as a speaking and listening activity, although the talk that might precede a reading is valid. It also follows that reading from a script or speaking from memory is not speaking and listening either.

A policy for speaking and listening in First Language English

Given the importance of speaking and listening and the large number of skills that it encompasses, it makes sense to discuss and establish:

- the part that speaking and listening should play in the work of students. Should all lessons or assignments include space for supervised discussion? What importance should you place on talk in pairs and solo presentation? Would you rather regard speaking and listening as a separate, 'bolt-on' activity?
- the method of assessment you should use, if any. Should it be formally examined or should you use an agreed form of self-assessment?
- the relationship of work in your department to that of other departments. Are there other teachers who use methods similar to those suggested in this chapter? If so, what can be done to support their work? Should there be a whole-school policy?

Starting from the beginning: *Do my students really need practice in speaking and listening? They have enough to say for themselves already.*

Maybe so, but there is a difference between informal talk and sustained task completion. Try using some of these exercises just to be sure. You are looking for clarity, confidence, a minimum of preparation and talking strictly without notes.

1 Give directions from school to … wherever.
2 Telephone someone to say that you cannot make an appointment and ask for another date.
3 Go to a shop and explain that an article they repaired still doesn't work.
4 Explain a particular function in computing to a novice.
5 Entertain a visitor to the school for five minutes until the head teacher is free.
6 Explain to the head teacher why you did something extremely silly, and apologise.
7 Give a two-minute talk to the class and answer questions.
8 Bring an article into school and persuade someone to buy it.

Teacher activity 2.1 (discussion)

Check activities 1 to 8 against the lists of skills and purposes (see page 10) to see what sorts of practice they give. What levels of ability might each activity demonstrate? Remember that any one activity may be applied to several skills and may touch on others.

Dealing with basic organisational problems in the classroom

The secret of speaking and listening (or listening, thinking and speaking) is to do plenty of it. Make it a habit and make your students aware that it is a part of the course, whether or not it is formally assessed for an examination. If your class size is under ten, you have few problems; if thirty, you have an organisational and time problem. The time problem is helped if you accept that most speaking and listening is not solo work but is done in pairs and small groups. If you want solo work, like giving talks, it is not necessary to ask everyone in the class to give one, or you could designate one to each lesson.

If students understand that talk is an essential part of English, they will probably settle down to an activity more easily. They will be used to working in pairs and will probably not even have to move places. In small groups, they can normally work with the same students each time and have the same position in the classroom. Thus movement is minimal.

Because of noise generated by excited talk, it is useful to put tables into an L-shape and have one student sitting in the angle and two opposite. There is much less chance of someone being ignored. Sitting in a straight line never works, because those on the end cannot hear what is going on.

The noise problem is best approached by using all corners of the classroom and by separating groups as much as possible. However, there always will be noise. You do not have to be like the head teacher who said to his English Department, 'By all means do speaking and listening, but I don't want to hear a sound, not a sound!'

Listed below are some common problems that arise during groupwork, together with possible solutions:

- Not everyone is involved – make the group size smaller, changing the seating, or giving cues to those who are not involved.
- Some of the groups are not working well, and there is a pecking order – tactfully change the members and ensure that the loudest and the busiest are not always in charge. Talk to the most active about a possible role in encouraging and bringing out the shy members of the group.
- Some groups treat an agenda of tasks as a list requiring the briefest of answers – ensure that items on the list are very open, never closed. It may be necessary to put someone who is adept at opening a discussion into the group to help the others.
- Someone is unkind to others whose comments they regard as silly – ensure that it is understood that everyone should be respected for what they say. It is right to argue a point, but not so that the original speaker feels a fool. Be tough on this.

Skills in performance – effective speaking and listening in small groups

Student activity 2.1 evaluating a poem

Teacher: We've read the poem. Now I want you to work in your groups and discuss these questions. What is the poem about? What is the mood of the poem and how do you know? What is the poet's attitude to the topic? How does the language and the way the poem is set out help you to answer the first three questions? You have fifteen minutes, and I want someone from each group to report back to us all.

Circulate in order to listen to what is said. Students are used to this and generally pay no attention. You might give occasional prompts, but you don't normally join in. Your body language indicates respect and interest, and they become confident in your presence. If you are aware of someone doing well, you may assess them.

| Teacher: | Thank you. I enjoyed listening to what you said and I |
| (after fifteen minutes, prompts) | would like group 1 to report back first. Ranjit? |

| Teacher: | Thank you, Ranjit. Now I heard group 3 talking about how they found the poem sad. Perhaps you could tell the class what you thought. |

After summarising the points, the poem is taught, but you spend five minutes finding out whether individuals liked the poem, and why.

You did not say, 'Discuss the poem'. They would not have known where to begin and would have wasted the fifteen minutes trying to agree on an agenda, or picking on bits of it at random and speaking to no purpose. It helped them to have your agenda which could be the same every time they studied a poem.

It would also be helpful if they knew the routine and were well trained in choosing someone to report back, not the same person every time.

It is best if you see your role as listener in group activities, though a simple prompt, perhaps only a few words, may save a discussion from stagnation. Your part comes in the whole-class session where you are eliciting sustained responses from individuals.

You might like to try these ploys for challenging students and for facilitating wider discussion:

'Thank you. I think I understood the point you were making, but it wasn't quite clear. Would you like to say it again in different words?'

'That is a good point. Did anyone else think that? Would you like to say it in your own words?'

'Yes, that is right. Can you give me an example?'

'Yes. Good. Go on. What else?'

'That was a great question you have just asked me. Would someone else like to answer it?'

This type of questioning is a confidence booster, involves people and makes them think effectively.

- Make a checklist of the different stages in the lesson described in Student activity 1.
- Look again at the objectives for speaking and listening at the beginning of this chapter. Which of the objectives are likely to be achieved during this lesson, and how?

Student activity 2.2 discussing dramatic effects

Teacher: We've just read Act 4, Scene 3, and we need to look at some of the dramatic effects. You remember what we said about dramatic effect last Thursday. So sort yourselves into three groups ... I'd like group 1 to act out the scene simply, just using Shakespeare's words. Group 2, I'd like you to do the first fifty lines in modern English. And group 3, I'd like you to mime the scene – no words please. Remember, you have got to make the audience react in the right places.

This is not an easy exercise, but it is one that students will work hard at, because they will look forward to seeing the scene from different angles. The talk that will take place is, as in Student activity 1, process talk, or talk that is a useful means to an end. You could assess groups 1 and 2 as they discussed the meanings of the words and the effects of those words on an audience. Group 2 would be searching for words that had a similar effect to Shakespeare's own. Group 3 would be discussing how Shakespeare's words could be translated into a mime. Each group would be appropriately challenged linguistically.

Process talk
What is process talk?
- It is part of the learning process associated with an assignment. Suppose that students are studying some poems. Because you are anxious that the learning should not be the result of a lecture or notes given by you, you insert into your lesson plan a timed and disciplined period of discussion which you can monitor, summing up what has happened to complete part of or the whole learning process.
- Through process talk, students learn about the topic.
- They also learn about their language – the challenge of the discussion tests their linguistic skills to the full.
- They do not speak from notes. The talk is ephemeral. Attempts to repeat it will usually be inferior.

- You save time because the assignment becomes more memorable and because the talk is a stepping stone to the end result – presumably, but not necessarily, some writing. In the case of Student activity 2, the intention may be simply to understand aspects of the scene.
- Although much of the talk may be halting or disjointed, some students will make their best contributions under these conditions.
- Using talk in this way, students share ownership of an assignment.

Using process talk to prepare for a writing assignment

Student activity 2.3	planning some directed writing

In this assignment, students have to plan some directed writing and then to select material from a number of articles to supplement what they already know.

Before they start, you warn them not to copy whole sentences from any resources they use. You tell them to make notes in their own words (see Chapter 4) and select what they think is important, so that no two pieces of writing appear the same.

Suppose the topic is 'Elephants'. It may be useful to show a video first (e.g. National Geographic). A video contains a vast amount of information and it is unlikely that students will choose the same bits. It is also virtually impossible for them to copy the spoken words.

Teacher: First of all, I want you to discuss the different aspects of the elephant and its life that you want to include in your writing: like family life, intelligence, whether the animal is dangerous or not, reserves, poaching or conservation. Talk together in groups and help each other to plan the content of your writing.

Student: Does everyone in the group have to do the same?

Teacher: No, it would be better if everyone followed their own ideas and interests, but I'd like you to help each other to think things out. You have ten minutes.

While this is going on, prepare to give each group a folder of articles – see below – and at the end of ten minutes …

Teacher: Now here are some articles, one (or two) for every member of the group. I'd like each person to read one and then give the rest of the group a summary of what it says. Say what interests you and how it might be helpful. Read your article quietly for about ten minutes. Then you will need about fifteen minutes to talk about what you have read.

They do this and then there is time for them to use the articles to supplement their own ideas.

The whole session will take up one normal lesson of about forty-five minutes. A lesson of an hour would allow planning and some first drafting at a leisurely rate.

This is another example of an assignment that is made up of reading, writing and speaking and listening, but at this point in the assignment it is speaking and listening that is playing the most important part.

Teacher activity 2.3 (discussion)

Make a checklist of all the skills that Student activity 3 covers. Which skills are specifically those of speaking and listening? How would you monitor students' performance and what sort of advice might you give them? It may help to have particular students that you teach in mind.

A note on resourcing

To resource this example, there is plenty of information available from the Internet. On one occasion, a search engine presented three interesting and informative sites:

- www.pbs.org/wnet/nature/elephants proved to be accessible, easy to navigate, and provided a number of resources. These included: 'life of the elephant', 'tale of the trunk' and 'poaching problems'. There was a long list of links and a bibliography.
- Another good site was www.elephants.com, an article on how elephants began, with a link to global news, and an up-to-date series of news links.
- www.nczooeletrack.org/diary/loomis-diary/index.html was less immediately useful, but offered a worthwhile and entertaining series of diary entries.

Further uses of process talk for issue-based assignments

You may wish to have students respond to worldwide or local matters that are controversial. In the first session, they will amass arguments for and against, and decide where they stand individually. This may lead to a mini-debate which can be presented to the class by one of the groups. The articles will be from newspapers and magazines. The Internet gives a wide choice of up-to-date newspaper access from the whole world, so you can choose your country of reference with less likelihood of bias. Local issues are often good to use since they may provoke more argument and are often easier to understand. If they touch on moral issues, the argument will be better.

Here are three real examples which have worked. They may not all be realistic in the country where you teach, but you can think of situations that are similar:

- A young person is refused an essential kidney operation because she has taken drugs. A national newspaper has splashed the story on its front page. Students read the article to discover the reasons for the decision and discuss the practical and moral issues.
- A student is excluded from a school because his appearance (in this case, his hairstyle) is unsuitable and against the school rules. His parents are very angry and call in the city newspaper. Students discuss the actions of the school and whether they are necessary.
- A town is shocked by a senseless case of bad driving which kills a popular young man. Students discuss their reactions and the problems faced by young drivers who have recently passed their tests.

Other examples of group talk

Media 1   Students analyse and evaluate the reporting of an incident or issue in more than one newspaper. They examine the factual reporting, the extent to which the news is made dramatic, sad or happy, the differences in language, the headlines, the amount of detail given, and so on.
End result   Analytical/critical writing

Media 2   Students plan and design a sales campaign for an item such as crocodile meat, a currently unfashionable garment, or a new type of mobile telephone. They decide how it is to be marketed, the consumers to be targeted, the message by which it will be sold, the content of any commercials and the design of newspaper and magazine advertisements. There is an oral report to the class.
End result   Informative/persuasive writing

Problem solving   Students decide on a group of people, for example the blind or the arthritic, whom they could help by designing some object. People could be approached to find out what everyday jobs they find most difficult. For example, one charity for the blind wrote back to say that their members felt unable to work in their gardens which they especially loved, while those suffering from arthritis had problems with door handles and with the safe boiling of a kettle. The students discuss how they could help and formulate a proposal with designs and an account of how the article could be made.

End result   Informative/explanatory writing

Brainstorming   This can be used to apply the mind to any problem. The rule is that no suggestion, however silly, is to be rejected.

Teacher activity 2.4 (planning)

Plan a lesson that consists largely of speaking and listening. Time the different parts of the lesson and be particularly aware of (a) how to use what is discussed in groups for the benefit of the whole class; (b) what speaking and listening skills can be addressed and enhanced; and (c) what the lesson will lead to.

Speaking and listening in pairs
Formality and informality

There are various degrees of formality in speaking and listening. Setting up a small group to deliver a stage in an assignment, particularly where reporting back or performing a role play, part of a play or a reading of a poem implies formality, since you are appearing before a group of listeners. Hence the definition of performance has very grey edges. You could argue that the stresses of talking or performing to a group as small as, for example, four are for some the same as those of appearing in front of the class or the whole school.

Pair talk is not normally formal.

Student activity 2.4   revision and practice

You teach a rule about grammar.

Teacher: Work with your partner for two or three minutes: I want the person on my left to explain the rule I have just taught. Your partner is to listen carefully and correct anything that is wrong or add bits that are missed out. Then both of you write a sentence that contains an example of the rule, read it to each other and decide which one would be better to read to the class.

Lessons are best understood by the person who teaches them! So the end result is consolidation and a quick check on anyone who has not understood. You won't assess anything here because it isn't sustained enough.

Student activity 2.5 planning a task together

This is a failsafe mechanism. It gives time for you to check that they know what to do and for them to iron out problems. They can agree on contexts for writing, develop characters in stories and discuss endings. It is sometimes useful to set tasks that can be presented in different ways: for example, some might want to answer in the form of a letter, others as a diary, while some tell a story. Discussion brings ownership.

Student activity 2.6 drafting

Person A reads Person B's first draft out loud, spots strengths such as good expression (choice of words) and weaknesses such as lack of clarity in the events of a story. The process is reversed and positive redrafting (see Chapter 4) takes place.

Student activity 2.7 conversation

A range of personal conversations could include matters concerning family life and discussions of moral and social issues, such as what you would do if:
- you saw someone commit a crime and it would be easier for you to pretend you hadn't;
- you made a remark you subsequently came to regret.

Conversations about school events, such as playing a part in the school play, being in a winning sports team or going on an outward bound expedition work well.

Student activity 2.8 role-played chat-show conversations

Examples are a host and a character from a book or play, two characters from a book or play talking to each other, two characters from different books or plays, a host and a person in the news or from history. A pitfall is that they may try to write a script. The best way is for the host not simply to ask questions, certainly not closed questions, but to play an important part in the conversation, giving prompts and opening out ideas. Prompts could be in note form but the other character would speak entirely without notes.

Student activity 2.9 | interviews

If appropriate, pairs could role play interviews for work. This activity forms a good groupwork session as well. Here three interviewers meet three interviewees and one is chosen at the end. Then the roles are reversed.

A note on role play

Role play is popular with students and some do it adroitly. However, invent situations that they recognise and can develop. Family and school situations are easy, perhaps a little too easy because they often descend into the stereotypical. Situations from literature and role plays involving characters are useful for understanding what students read, and such exercises are accessible since the necessary material is in the book. It is more difficult to play a manager of a shop when you have never stopped to consider how a manager acts and thinks. Such role plays often go round in circles. Above all, never let students write scripts for role plays. For assessment, you will have more material if you listen to the planning and the very first run-through. You are the best judge of whether role play works with your students. You will soon spot any weaknesses and learn to avoid them.

Whole-class discussion

You can teach informally with students sitting in a circle without tables. In fact, you may have better control of the situation when no one is at the back or the front and there is no opportunity to hide behind the furniture. You sacrifice the ability to write, but since the tables are against the walls, students can easily turn their chairs to start writing. Sitting like this, students know that you mean the session to be interactive and that they have to join in. The bigger the class the more may opt out, but the active, sustained participation of even two or three will make the lesson more interesting than just listening to you!

Student activity 2.10 | story endings

Hand out short story.

Teacher: I'm going to read you this short story. There are only two characters in it. Can I have two volunteers to read their dialogue? *(You start reading, but stop just before you turn over the last page.)* How do you think it is going to end and why?

Students A, B, C and D give suggestions while others argue for one solution or another.

Teacher: Now turn the page and we shall read the rest. *(Finish story.)* Were you surprised?

Students compare the ending with theirs (it may or may not be 'better', i.e. be more surprising, have more of a climax, have a stronger moral twist. They might talk about realism.)

Teacher: What does this tell you about writing an ending to a story?

Students talk about various effects in fiction.

Teacher: Sum up what the story has contributed to our understanding of how fiction works.

In this lesson you are strongly in control of the outcome, but the discussion is student centred. They may not particularly approve of the ending, although you have probably chosen a story with a trick ending anyway. If you repeat the lesson a fortnight later, they will be well clued up when you turn over the last page, or you can look at a different aspect of the short story such as the beginning, or how much information you are given about the characters and their background. In time, this will lead to better fiction writing from at least some of the class.

Solo work

For some schools, this is what constitutes speaking and listening. Students must stand up in front of an audience and try their best to entertain them for some minutes. While this is laudable, it should only be a part of a varied programme of speaking and listening. However, careers may depend on the ability to stand up to train a group of new workers, to give a presentation in front of managers, or to persuade customers to buy a gimmicky machine in the local market. Sometimes there are prestigious local public-speaking or debating competitions entered by perhaps a few of your students.

Giving talks

You have to consider whether it is kind to put all students through this exercise, although you can, of course, give training in formal speaking. On the other hand, some of your students will be keen to tell you about hobbies and special abilities and, in doing so, will add to their self-confidence and to the enjoyment of their class. Two examples of these are one student who looked after the chickens on his father's farm and, at the age of eleven, kept a class spellbound for 35 minutes; and another, aged fifteen, who went hill racing on his motorcycle every weekend, and was an expert at taking it to pieces and putting it together. His talk lasted 40 minutes and was his greatest achievement in English.

Let those who have something interesting to say do it for the enjoyment of others. However, why put students through misery if all they can say is that they went to Spain for their holiday and sat by the swimming pool and turned rich pink for a whole week?

Other ways of making formal presentations

- Some students speak with interest and enthusiasm about their work experience, and perhaps the English department is the best place for debriefing.
- It's also a good exercise to get students to reteach a lesson they have recently had in another subject. It gives the opportunity to ask questions of the others. Beware: the rest of the class sometimes know the lesson better than their 'teachers'.
- You can also substitute the word 'presentation' for talk. Students can learn to use the overhead projector or even computerised presentation techniques. Presentations can be given in pairs.
- Try disputations, where one student speaks against another, maybe quite simply arguing the superiority of one spare-time obsession against another.
- Use traditional debates, but not too formally, and try to make the wording of the motion sound realistic and up to date.

 LOOKING BACK

- ◆ Has this chapter changed your perception of the importance of speaking and listening?
- ◆ Are there any changes to your practice that you would now consider making?
- ◆ How can you best offer opportunities and advice that will help students develop their skills as speakers and listeners?
- ◆ Are there any problems associated with the freedom of students to express their own views about what they are taught? If so, how should these be addressed?
- ◆ Are you worried about the amount of time that speaking and listening can take up? How would you address this?
- ◆ If you are not formally assessing your students in speaking and listening for an exam, how can you best persuade them of the importance of practising these skills?

3 Reading

Despite the Internet, sales of books and newspapers show no signs of falling. Book prizes still excite a high degree of media attention. Newspapers boast incredible circulations and, whatever your interest, you will find magazines to satisfy it. Nothing has yet replaced books and newspapers as reading material. Television gives information in another form and leaves nothing to the imagination when telling stories. The Internet is a different sort of tool, in some ways quite cumbersome to use and posing potentially considerable reading difficulties for the user.

So it is still the teacher's responsibility to promote 'old-fashioned' reading and to encourage all students to make the effort. Of course, if you are a quick, fluent reader and have a good memory for what you read, you are more likely to enjoy reading. If it takes you a quarter of an hour to read every word as a separate item on a page, then you will probably be at least upset at your non-achievement and at worst will pronounce that all reading is nonsense: we all have computers, probably for playing games.

The skills for reading

You will remember the list of objectives from Chapter 2:

1 understand information;
2 select what is relevant to specific purposes and collate information within and between texts;
3 appreciate the difference between facts, ideas and opinions;
4 recognise implicit meanings and attitudes;
5 evaluate information and detect bias;
6 appreciate a writer's use of language.

Objectives 1, 2, 3 and 5 cover reading skills associated with what is often still called 'comprehension', while Objectives 4 and 6 cover most reading skills associated with the study of literature. These could be expanded as follows:

- Objective 4 (variation) – understand literary texts beyond their literal meanings in terms of the issues and attitudes they raise;

- Objective 6 (variation) – recognise and appreciate the ways in which writers use language to create their effects of narration, description, characterisation and literary structure.

The following list shows how students can develop their thinking skills in fulfilling objectives for reading:
- Students **analyse** texts to pick out information, examples of writers' attitudes and linguistic effects.
- They **synthesise** by collating material within and between texts.
- They **evaluate** by commenting on the effectiveness of a media text or the opinions expressed in an extreme article, or expressing their preference (with reasons) for one poem over another.

There are also skills that are connected with the mechanics of reading, for example:
- reading aloud fluently and with expression;
- silent reading effectively and at speed;
- skimming for gist;
- scanning for detail.

A policy for reading in First Language English
The place of reading in the English curriculum
When you decide on what the general work of the department should be based, you have three alternatives:
1 to base your work mostly on texts chosen by you from which you form your assignments and demonstrate writing skills in different genres;
2 to work from a coursebook for some of the time and supplement what you do with texts chosen by yourself;
3 to work entirely from coursebooks (understanding that reading will be in the form of tantalisingly short extracts).

Option 1 is satisfying but hard work. Option 3 is easy, but can be frustrating and may take you in directions that do not entirely fit your style of teaching.
   A decision also has to be taken about the types and variety of texts that students read and work from. These could be:

novels and short stories	biographies	newspapers
plays	travel literature	advertising
poems	letters	magazines
	propaganda	websites

They represent a great deal of reading and study, and some care is required in managing students' total reading experience.

A respect for where the student is

You will want to be aware of the progress of each student in the class. The department has to handle the problem of poorer readers who know their limitations and need your acknowledgement of them and the belief that they can and will improve. You may have a policy for helping students to improve by using other adults, older students or other students in the class.

A policy for designating time for reading

Do you agree with silent reading time in class, when you can be sure that reading is taking place and when you can monitor what students are reading? Should this time be spent in the library or should work in the library consist of something different? Is reading aloud in class important, and how should it be organised to make it effective?

Reading records

Do you think they have a place and, if so, what form should they take? Should they just be dates and titles, or do you require some sort of a response to be added. Should they be part of a wider self-assessment document for reading? To what age are they useful, or could a more complex document be used for older classes?

Note-taking

Although a writing activity, note-taking is normally associated with reading and provides valuable evidence of the individual's ability to understand. What styles of note-taking should be taught, and how should students choose which form is best for them?

Teacher activity 3.1 (discussion)

Without recourse to documentation, discuss your departmental reading policy. Is there one, or can everyone teach as they wish? Do you remember and practise your policy? Do you need to revise your present policy? What could be done to help other departments – or obtain help – by discussing reading policy with them?

Reading in other departments

When you are satisfied with your own reading policy, you can share it with other interested teachers. For example, you might agree on the ways in which texts are used in class in other subjects. Some students may not be able to cope alone with a chapter in, say, a biology textbook unless there is an agreed way in which they proceed. Note-taking could therefore become a school policy and save a lot of hassle. You could share some of the ways in which students respond to what they read with your colleagues. Visiting some of their lessons could be an eye-opener, and you might adopt their techniques as well as making suggestions.

Reading in the first three years of the secondary school – checking and developing basic skills

When faced with a weak or reluctant reader, it is easy to assume that your colleagues in the junior school have not done their job well. In fact, much time and effort will have gone into reading, although there will still be students who have difficulties. A good starting point is to check for warning signs without the effort of resorting to standardised tests:

- Hear everyone read aloud. Give them something easy. The best readers will confidently show their fluency and will use emphasis and tone of voice. The worst readers will read word by word.
- Ask everyone to read silently. After five minutes, tour the class and make a check on how far everyone has read. Do the same five minutes later. By this time you will know where the average reader is and who are the quickest – not necessarily the best – and the slowest.
- Ask the slowest readers to tell you what they have read. Check whether they give a gist or retell the whole story in detail. Ask the quickest readers last of all. Check that they really know what they have read since some let their eyes race over the words. You may therefore find that slow readers are, in a way, the most effective.

In this next stage, students practise mechanical reading skills and skills of understanding.

| Student activity 3.1 | eye-watch |

Students work in pairs, taking it in turns to read silently. The second student watches the eyes of the first as they move along the lines. 'Good' readers read methodically; their eyes normally sweep over half a line at a time, pausing briefly in the middle and at the end. 'Poor' readers' eyes move erratically, word by word or two words at a time, and may also move backwards and forwards along the line. Some readers may go back over sections of the page they have read before.

The second student monitors this and reports back. Students who have been reading erratically may be able to correct the fault with a little effort and thus improve the speed of their reading.

Student activity 3.2 | gist

Give students a page to find and, as soon as they do so, tell them to start reading, say the first two pages. How much will depend on the way the story unwinds. You need an event for them to reach. Say you will give them one minute only, and time it exactly. At the end of the minute, ask them to summarise the story, without concern for details. You will find most can do it reasonably well, but also that they will be confused about the relationship of detail to main events. Slower readers may surprise themselves. The main point to make is the speed at which the brain works.

Student activity 3.3 | speed reading

Ask students to read the first sentence of a paragraph carefully for meaning and then cast the eye down the rest of the paragraph to see how much of the subsequent material makes an effect.

Student activity 3.4 | fast-time comprehension

- Choose a suitable short article or a part of a story.
- Say to the class, 'Find page 27' (or whatever).
- Almost immediately, start asking questions such as, 'Where did the Black Death originate?'
- Students scan the page until they see 'Black Death' and 'originate', complete the sentence in the book and a forest of hands shoots up with the answer, 'China'.
- Vary the difficulty by changing words, such as, 'Where did the Black Death start?' but making the clues less obvious will not greatly affect the response.

You will be surprised at the speed with which answers are given, since there has been no time to study the passage. It shows how fast the brain scans a text for information (think of the speed of an Internet search engine).

There's a cautionary tale here. If you want to test reading for information by simple location questions such as the one about the Black Death, you will save time if you do not ask students to write down the answers. Easy comprehension is better done orally. You can probably think of other ways to present this exercise, such as to read the passage aloud and get the class to shout out the number of the question when they come to the appropriate answer.

Reading a text in class

The standard of reading will be so high in some classes that students are able effectively to prepare a chapter for discussion in very little time. However, in many cases, you will wish to ensure that the reading is clearly understood and that there is plenty of practice in using reading skills. You could therefore arrange for the reading of a chapter of a book in class so that there is variety and interest, and so that weaker readers are not unreasonably left behind.

| Student activity 3.5 | group and solo reading |

Read the beginning of the story aloud for no more than five to ten minutes. This gives a good start and you can stop reading at a moment of high interest. Two quick class questions or a comment from you will cue them into the next part of the reading.

The class divides into reading groups, formed by you, to include good, average and at least one poor reader in each group. The groups continue to read aloud and the reading is allocated so that a poor reader has sufficient practice but does not hold the group up. Someone in the group will assist the poor reader where necessary. The teacher monitors the progress of each group in the reading. Allow ten to fifteen minutes. Bring the story summary up to date. You may ask how the story might proceed from this point, so that students could make inferences from earlier clues.

The rest of the story is read silently. When it is finished, ask someone to summarise the whole story (a test of selecting material and understanding and conveying information).

Alternatives

You can read to the class with the help of students. For example, you read a long paragraph and someone else reads a short one, or students take part in dialogue, playing different characters. Mechanical reading round the class rarely works. They need someone to hold it together and to conduct.

Skills in performance
How to tell whether a text is easy or difficult
The difficulty of a text is roughly indicated by the length and complexity of the sentences and the density of the vocabulary in terms of three-syllable words. Of course, some sentences of 20 words may be much denser than others. For example, sentences which are largely joined by 'and' make fewer demands on the reader. Other sentences have complex structures made more difficult by practices such as collapsing clauses into various forms of phrase. Some texts may be rich in common three-syllable words such as 'difficult' or 'horrible', while others may draw on a much wider range of vocabulary or use specialised words as in mathematics and science. Some short words like 'edge' may give difficulty.

A reason why two texts of apparently equal difficulty may not pose the same obstacles is that of interest. A student reading an engaging topic may find it easier than a 'boring' text, especially if it is set out well in a friendly font size with attractive pictures.

When a student chooses a book to read, you can easily use these methods to assess its suitability and, by monitoring the level of difficulty, prevent a sense of failure. Remember that poor readers sometimes perversely choose difficult books.

Using books in the classroom
Providing time in class for students to select books and to read silently was mentioned earlier as a feature in a departmental reading policy. To put this into action you will need one of the following:

- a large and varied book box, preferably of new books. Students will not warm to a collection of books with pages missing and which are cracking at the spine. The books are normally all different titles, but it is possible to have a general reading programme with several copies of, say, a dozen titles.
- access to the library with permission given to you to sign books out on your own register. This will provide more books and you will not have the expense of providing a book box. Some librarians are prepared to issue book boxes from stock to your classroom.

Do not forget that some students will prefer non-fiction to fiction and that some tact is needed in dealing with this.

Silent reading does not have much point unless there are active outcomes.

Student activity 3.6   **book recommendation 1**

Students talk about a book they have read. They introduce the story, read a paragraph or so that they like and give recommendations for others to read the book. Others ask questions to see whether they might like the book as well.

This gives practice in understanding and conveying information, selecting what is interesting to the audience and making evaluations. It is likely that some of the questions may lead to recognising implicit meanings and attitudes. Where you recognise these skills in action, you may intervene to allow a student to develop a train of thought.

Student activity 3.7   **book recommendation 2**

Students write about a page, single- or double-sided, recommending a book they have read.

The page can include:
- a small section of the story;
- 'my favourite character';
- whether it is good for older or younger students;
- a picture;
- reasons why the book should be read.

These pages are bound in two or three folders which are left in the book box or available to the class when they visit the library. You will find that it becomes a popular feature.

An alternative is to make the writing of the pages the basis of an Internet exchange with a school in another part of the world.

Again, this activity fulfils most of the skill-based objectives, particularly those of recognising implicit meaning in making personal statements about characters and evaluating the book. All these skills can be practised simply at an early age and developed to a much higher level as the students mature and progress.

Student activity 3.8   **cover design**

Students design book covers, including a brief publisher's 'blurb' to go on the back cover. This is more of a media exercise and is meant for classroom display to increase awareness of book reading. Other artistic assignments include pictures of characters which can be displayed with a selection of keywords that describe them.

Student activity 3.9 performing scenes from a book

Small groups perform short play scenes based on a section of a book. If only one person has read the book, the story will have to be told and the group will have to understand the background and the characters. There will also have to be a spoken introduction before the scene is performed. Even if there is only one copy, they can still read out the portion they are going to act. If you use a book box with several copies of titles, this activity is made easier. Final performances can be recorded on video.

There are many possibilities in this work. It calls for careful understanding of the text and an interpretation of character and the significance of events. Particular attention has to be given to speaking dialogue, since the tone of voice will reveal implicit meanings. There are also possibilities for discussion of how different characters are made to speak, and why. There are frequent sections of text where close comprehension is essential for characters to be correctly portrayed.

Student activity 3.10 inviting a writer to visit a class

There may be a scheme whereby writers can be booked to talk about and present their work or run writing workshops, or you may be able to invite a writer through a website. An alternative is to invite a local adult writer, although you would have to be clear about the quality of their work first. A third alternative is to invite someone like a journalist who is a professional writer but does not write fiction.

Some writers are excellent at holding students' attention and letting them into the secrets of writing in an interesting way. Others can be a disaster, so you take a risk unless you work through recommendation.

Student activity 3.11 fancy-dress party

Students attend a fancy-dress party dressed as a character from a book they have read.

Student activity 3.12 book week

You hold a book week throughout the school. This can be linked to other schools and organisations in the locality. This would be an opportunity to invite a writer celebrity or visitors from your town or city to talk about what reading means to them.

Plan a book week to be held throughout the school.

Student activity 3.13 self-assessment documents

These go beyond simple lists of books that have been read and encourage students to think about their reading and their reading skills. You can construct them to fulfil whatever purposes you have for them; the example given below is only one possibility. It could be in two parts so that the running record of what has been read would be with the student all the time while the self-assessment questions might only be issued once or twice a year.

- Write a list of what you have read this term. Do not include books that you did not read for more than a few pages.
- What did you like best? Why?
- What did you like least? Why?
- When do you enjoy reading the most?
- Complete this sentence: When I have to read aloud to others …
- My reading has improved this term in the following ways:
- I still have to improve …
- I feel very confident/confident/average/not very confident/very unconfident about reading.
- Who has helped you the most this term with your reading? Friend/teacher/relative/someone else.
- Any comment you would like to make to your teacher/parent etc.
- Space for parent's comments.

Using books in the library

It is helpful to be timetabled for library work so that students can find out where books are and how to access information. A number of examples of activities in the library are included here.

Student activity 3.14 where to find information

Start with the reference section and how to use an encyclopedia. Then look at other sections such as applied science, social studies, biography and geography. Show them where books on hobbies are. Teach them to look for clues to separate easy books from difficult books.

Student activity 3.15   how to find information from a book

This is an advanced reading skill, requiring skim reading, selection and the specific skill of using indexes effectively. They will need to understand how to use:

- contents lists – for example, they are researching famous people's schooldays to see whether they were successes or failures, and are using biographies. Most of the contents lists direct them specifically to schooldays.
- indexes – they need practice in thinking of appropriate index headings – the information may be in the book, but not where they are searching. They also need to be aware that some references will only give them a single piece of information, whereas one that covers several pages may be the main reference to that topic.
- picture cues – usually, but not always, there will be text associated with a picture.

They also need a reminder that skimming and scanning will help them to over-read a section quickly and to locate keywords.

Student activity 3.16   short-term projects

These can be written or spoken. You need to avoid the possibility of copying whole sections of books. The use of note-taking largely avoids this, particularly if the time given to researching is short. Examples are:

- a story to be written about someone growing up in Hong Kong. The student finds good references in two encyclopedias and in a short, descriptive book in the geography section. Information is selected and collated, and the result is an adventure story which culminates in a chase between two powerful boats. There is plenty of recognisably local colour.
- a talk about the life of two famous women of the last century. Again, the student starts by using encyclopedias and supplements knowledge by reading sections of two biographies.

Student activity 3.17   groupwork

Each person in the group researches a different text on the same topic and is responsible for relaying information to the group leader, who compiles and orders the information.

You have been timetabled for five lessons in the library. Decide which year should be involved and discuss how you would best like to use the time. Briefly plan the content of each lesson.

Note-taking

This is a skill in itself, but it involves a complexity of skills of understanding facts, ideas and opinions, of selection and of evaluation. The task of selecting a small amount of material from a normal-sized book is challenging. Reading skills such as skimming and scanning are essential in note-taking.

Two methods of note-taking are described below – spider diagrams and traditional note-taking with headings.

Start by demonstrating **spider diagrams**. Show students how to start from the middle with a box with the title of the topic inside. Then every time they find something relevant, they should write it down and attach it by a line to the centre. They should go on doing this, travelling round the page until they have run out of reading matter. If they find ideas that are like each other, they should make sure that these are attached to the same line of thought. Tell students to include in their notes only what they understand.

Spider diagrams very rarely lead to copying from the text and are very flexible as far as order is concerned.

Traditional notes consist of headings which are best chosen by the note-taker, and brief notes, usually in lists rather than sentences, under the headings. Much work can be done to show how to lay the notes out effectively. While keywords are probably copied from the original, the aim is to avoid copying whole phrases and sentences. Notes should be, as far as possible, in the students' own words.

They may need to use:
- headings and subheadings;
- number systems for lists;
- bullets;
- icons;
- indentations.

Students choose which of these forms they want to use and are encouraged to personalise their system of note-taking.

Pitfalls of note-taking

Some students will not accept that notes should be short, will not cut down sentences and will produce many pages of notes, expecting your praise. They should be monitored while making their notes.

There are no pitfalls connected with spider diagrams, which can be developed in several ways and which reflect the informal nature of note-taking. They can easily be used by less able students to great effect.

Researching using CD-ROMs and the Internet

It is essential that students understand:

- the sheer pointlessness and danger of reproducing articles and information from a CD-ROM or the Internet and pretending that it is their own – plagiarism is becoming much easier to detect!
- the difficulties of locating useful websites and searching them for information that is truly useful to them;
- that reading and making notes directly from a monitor screen is quicker than reading from a printed copy, and also use less paper.

As an example of an exercise, use a CD-ROM encyclopedia that gives sufficient detail to give simple note-making exercises for facts and explanations about:

- turtles and tortoises;
- Iraq;
- the bicycle;
- hair;
- the Egyptian pyramids.

In some encyclopedias, topics include a list of headings which can be used as additional references.

It is more complicated to work off websites. It is hard to make useful judgements when reading the list supplied by a search engine. For example, there is confusion between selling and giving information. Try finding information on bicycles via a search engine. Once you make your choice and download, it may not give you much information, or it may prove difficult to navigate the website.

| Student activity 3.18 | Internet research |

Use a search engine to research Roald Dahl. You will find:
- www.roalddahlfans.com;
- www.roalddahl.org, the official website.

It will be hit and miss as to which pages you really need. However, in general when using websites, the biography is a starting point, and the official website has sound information and includes an interview. It might be a good idea for students to log the difficulties they have in accessing the information they want. Another good strategy is to help students list the type of information they want before using the search engine.

The reading skills involved here are as advanced as those needed for selecting relevant information from a book. When using the Internet, one is rarely aware of just how much reading is taking place. Students are recommended to learn how to collate information from more than one website and to acknowledge where the information has come from.

Helping students develop their reading skills from the computer may occupy a good deal of time. Remember that you must prevent mindless copying of what has been discovered. Printing an article is very easy, but it is worth encouraging students to make their notes from the screen.

Reading in the examination years
Reading resources
Some teachers prefer all the reading that goes on in class to be literary. If you confine the reading in this way, you limit the experience your students have of working with different types of written communication. The range of reading should therefore include:
- informative texts;
- persuasive texts (argument, polemic);
- media texts (advertising, newspapers, the Internet);
- literary texts (stories, novels, plays, poems);
- biography and autobiography;
- travel literature.

It is also a very rewarding study to read texts that reflect many different cultures. There are many recent short stories that deal with original, interesting and controversial ideas. In international schools, the multicultural make-up of each class can be acknowledged.

Textual analysis
This involves the reading of short texts which should reflect the variety of genres indicated above. For example, one day they might read a personal letter and a business letter; your next choice might be a newspaper report of a local incident; then perhaps, a famous speech and, finally in this section, a set of instructions. Another group of texts might be the opening of a story, a short scene from a play, a poem and a short piece of literary criticism.

Texts are read for meaning (both explicit and implicit), for discussion of the type and choice of language, and for learning about technical matters such as punctuation, paragraphing, sequence and grammar (in fact, all those things that were contained in the skill-based objectives).

Students will learn that the type of language used in a poem is not always suitable for a short story, and that the language used in a short story is very different from that used in a newspaper 'story'. They will also learn that a story can be conveyed through speech alone, so that many levels of meaning are conveyed in the dialogue of a play. Such a study may prompt them to use dialogue in stories more carefully and to some purpose.

| **Student activity 3.19** | analysing a literary text |

Take a literary example from *Of Mice and Men*, Chapter 2, starting with 'The bunkhouse was a long, rectangular building', and ending with 'Just says "gimme my time" one night, the way any guy would'.

Students help you with or take over the reading (the book is, after all a mixture of a story and a play).

What happens in the text?
(There is a description of the bunkhouse interior in the sunshine, thrown into life by the opening of the latch and the entry of the old man, George and Lennie, and a conversation about a man who has left.)

(a) Teacher: What's special about the description? Draw it. Why was that easy? Now discuss words chosen to give precise meaning, not generality. Any words you didn't know? After all they aren't long words (they don't have to be, do they). Whitewash? Burlap? Scoff? Vials? Sceptically? Bristly?

   Teacher: Now look at the way Steinbeck introduces movement into the still life. What details give movement to the scene?

(b) Teacher: Look at the conversation. What does it add to what you already know? Do you think the bunkroom was a dirty place? Did it really have bugs? ...

   Teacher: What does the conversation tell you about George and the old man – and Whitey?

Teacher: Now draw up your own impressions of the old man. Use information from the moment the door opens to the end of the passage. Use your own words as far as possible. Don't confuse facts about his appearance with his character and personality. Can you draw information about him from the way he speaks?

Word study

Teacher: Compare the language of the first eighteen lines with that of the last eighteen. Look at the words, look at the grammar. Talk about writing standard English and about imitating the language of real speech.

Paragraphing

This text is divided into eleven paragraphs, some long, some short. Discuss the reasons for starting paragraphs in these places.

Punctuation

Dictate a small section of the conversation (e.g. the two contributions from '"I don't know," said the old man.'). Tell them to add punctuation. They check from the text and discuss. Also talk about use of dashes, three dots and the apostrophe (which always means that there is a letter missing, even if the reasons are far in the past). In the first paragraph, there is much work to do with commas, and you will find a semicolon.

Grammar

Look how the first paragraph starts with short sentences and gradually uses more complicated structures. In sentence 4, look at the use of 'made-up' and 'showing'. Look at the use of 'so that it showed' as a connective. Discuss how it is sometimes all right to use 'and' to start sentences and discuss the reason here. Look at consistently accurate use of participles such as 'stove-pipe going', 'table littered'; also, 'around it were grouped'.

Spelling

You will know which words your own particular students spell wrongly. A short test of the following words might be in order:

building	wooden	personal
occupant	medicines	shoulder
mattress	carefully	neighbouring
finally		

You dictate the words and the students check and correct by rereading the text. They learn corrections thus:

- look at the word;
- say the word;
- write it from memory.

When dictating words for spelling tests, it is helpful to say the word and then to put it in the context of two or three other words, or as the word was used in the text.

You can find a great amount to do in any text, although this is more complex than many. If you follow this sort of pattern (and add a piece of original writing such as, 'Write your own description of a still place with no people – then add an interloper'), you will have touched on many of the objectives upon which this book is based.

LOOKING BACK

- ◆ The start of the twenty-first century makes more reading demands on individuals, not fewer. How can you best ensure that each of your students can cope well with those demands, particularly with university and the world of work ahead? It is worth discussing what differences the Internet has made to our lives and what demands it makes on our reading skills.
- ◆ Another topic for discussion is the breadth of the reading experience students are expected to encounter. How do you wish to provide that breadth?

4 Writing

Just as we found in the case of reading, there is no evidence that the advent of the electronic age has lessened the need for communication via the written word, or the skills with which we communicate. Electronic devices such as spellcheckers and the thesaurus help those who know what they are doing, but leave those who don't in a worse state than before. Managers no longer have secretaries and are often assessed on the number of problems they can solve by letter. Emails are dashed off in a moment and can cause disastrous misunderstandings and become unexpectedly public property.

So the demands made on our writing skills are greater than ever before, and students are expected to have a broader experience of writing. No longer do we just write stories and essays, neither of which normally takes up the majority of our adult writing time unless they are our profession or our pastime.

The skills and purposes of writing

Once more, you will remember the list of objectives in Chapter 2:
1 articulate experience and express what is thought, felt and imagined;
2 order and present facts, ideas and opinions;
3 use language and register appropriate to audience and context;
4 exercise control of appropriate grammatical structures;
5 understand and use a range of apt vocabulary;
6 demonstrate an awareness of the conventions of paragraphing, sentence structure, punctuation and spelling.

The purposes for writing are:
1 to **inform**, explain and describe;
2 to **argue**, persuade and instruct;
3 to **explore**, imagine and entertain;
4 to **analyse**, review and comment.

These fall roughly into the categories of (1) informative and (2) argumentative writing, (3) writing stories and (4) the type of writing used for literature and media studies.

The general purpose of a piece of writing affects the language and, sometimes, the structure. A writer may intend to intimidate or to make the reader sympathise or be angry, or use bias, half-truths or propaganda, or swamp the reader with exaggerated language.

A policy for writing in First Language English

You will need to:

- be clear about the balance between giving students free reign to express themselves in writing, and teaching and insisting on technical matters such as spelling, punctuation and grammar;
- discuss ways in which you can offer students a wide range of writing experiences and help them to understand the reasons for practising writing in different genres and contexts and for different audiences;
- decide how students are to progress individually as writers during their years in the school;
- decide ways in which writing can be celebrated, for example in class and school publications, displays, competitions and events, such as a drama-writing week.

Skills in performance
Creating content

Are there any skills that can be developed to help students improve the content of writing tasks? In the classroom, you may use stimulus material, such as reading part of a story and then saying, 'now write the ending,' or 'write another adventure of the character you have been reading about.' One way of teaching the skill of inventing content without the direction of stimulus material is to incorporate what one would see, hear, smell, touch or taste into the writing.

Student activity 4.1	using the senses

Teacher: Look out of the window ... or round the classroom ... what exactly can you see? Shapes? Colours? What shades of red? Sit very quietly. What can you **hear**? (and perhaps **smell**, or **touch** – and, less likely, **taste**?) Now make your notes into one or two paragraphs. Try to write about a side. Use the present or the past tense, but not both!

Another skill is to use and to improve on memory, which is probably what imagination really is. Too many young writers imagine the improbable or even the impossible, and write immature stories of death and destruction. It is more skilful to use real people, places and events as the basis for writing. That is different from slavishly reproducing something that really happened, perhaps an incident that is too ordinary and lacking in detail in the memory to grab the attention of the reader. Suppose that students remember a real event and change the outcome into something far more interesting and unusual.

| Student activity 4.2 | using memory |

Teacher: Now **imagine**, but I really mean **remember**, a place that is very well known to you (like the view from your window at home, your favourite room in your house, your own street) and describe it as if you were really there. What details can you see? Shapes? Colours? What shades? Write about a side and a half.

Writing diaries is a useful way of combining techniques of describing things from memory by means of the five senses, combined with re-creating actual events. Here, younger students become used to re-creating actual events vividly and can incorporate how they felt about what happened.

| Student activity 4.3 | using a diary |

Teacher: We're going to write diaries. Not every day, but just when something important or unusual happens. It might be your birthday or a day out with your grandfather. Or perhaps you cooked something new and special at home, or St Helena won the World Cup. Or you saw something in a shop window that you really wanted, but couldn't possibly have now. Perhaps someone was happy or sad because of something you said or did. Perhaps it was something you saw which stuck in your mind. It doesn't have to be earth shattering, just a memory. Use your five senses to capture it in words before it fades away like a dream. Perhaps it was a dream. Don't write about a whole day. Concentrate on what was special. I guess the entries will be different lengths, but if they're less than half a side, I suppose there won't be enough detail to make them come to life. Remember that you need description to make events vivid. This assignment will last two months and I'll give you time in class to catch up with yourselves.

If students are used to using their active imaginations, that is re-creating people, places and events that are like those in their own memories, then they can bring narratives to life. Here are two examples of openings to a story about the apparently mundane experience of an examination day.

Version 1:

> Once upon a time there was a sixteen-year-old girl called Greta who lived with her ageing parents in a little wooden house on the outskirts of a town. Greta knew that her parents wanted most of all that she should pass her final examinations with flying colours, but she was a girl who found it hard to concentrate on anything much. Today was the day of the first examinations, and she had to admit that she had little confidence in herself ...

Or could it be like this?

Version 2:

> Greta woke with a shock. The rain was rattling against her attic window, her mind was still in her dreams and reality was only dawning on her in fragments. She yawned, pulling the bedclothes over her head. Then she remembered. Examinations! She had meant to get out of bed much earlier than, what was it? Ten past eight! That's what her watch said, and her first exam started at nine.

Teacher activity 4.1 (discussion)

If two of your students wrote these openings, what would you say to them, and why? The writer of version 1 would argue that the work was accurate and just as good as version 2. Could these examples form the basis for a lesson on beginnings?

Version 1 demonstrates skills of expression. It is accurately written, in order and fluent, and the vocabulary is reasonable if staid. Amazingly, people do write stories about passing and failing examinations, and there are many students who still feel that you have to begin at the beginning.

Version 2 gives you different information from version 1. The reader probably does have to know about where she lived and what her parents thought about her, but does that information have to come here? In fact, this story could start at one minute to nine as Greta arrived at school, or even the moment when the invigilator said, 'Put your pens down.'

Before we leave Greta to success or misery, let's think about the ending, the day on which the results come out. Our first writer's version is:

> On the day of the publication of the results, Greta made her way to school and read the notices posted in the window. With a sigh of relief, she realised that she had passed every subject. How her parents would be pleased!

Even the exclamation mark is correct.

The second version is:

> The day Greta had been dreading had arrived. Her mother kept on casting nervous little glances at her until she could not put it off any more. 'Good luck,' she whispered. Yes, Greta thought to herself, she needed it. She could hear the excited sounds of voices before she turned into the school gates. In front of her she could see the other girls. Three of her friends were dancing in a ring and hugging each other, but another had turned away from the display and was standing by herself with her hand over her mouth. As she drew nearer, her breathing became short and nervous and she could no longer see clearly. Would her name be there? Would she be able to find it, or stand there like a dummy unable to read? She seemed to hear her name but could not bear to look at anyone. She walked forward, nearer, right up to the glass. Her name came up to meet her.

It is a brave writer who leaves the story at this point, not telling the reader what comes next.

Getting things in order

Everybody knows about beginnings, middles and ends. The problem is getting them in the right proportions, and there is a special problem with non-narrative writing when students run out of material and repeat themselves, so that the argument goes round and round.

Paragraphs

Structure starts with paragraphs. Make sure that students understand the importance of a paragraph, that it has a topic sentence (that can go at the beginning or the end) and that there is some device that links it to the previous paragraph. Look at the example in the following activity.

The trouble with maps and directions in general is that what is on the page is very difficult to translate into what you see ahead of you through your car windscreen. The map you have been given is a series of little sticks, and the number of streets before you are due to turn left or right is never the same in reality. These little sticks may have route numbers, but when you reach the turn, the route number has mysteriously disappeared. You are left with a map that simply does not give you enough information to get you to your destination.

On the other hand, maps can be helpful if they give you clear and indisputable directions. For example, you may be told to 'take the first turn right after the roundabout'. Another set of directions advises you to 'go under the motorway bridge, carry on straight past the shops on either side of the road, cross the canal, and you will see the hotel on the left'. By using landmarks in this way, your journey can be made stress free.

Try rearranging the sentences and asking students to put them in the right order and tell you why they have done it that way. Draw their attention to the link between the two paragraphs and to sequencing devices such as 'for example', 'another', 'by using landmarks in this way'. Ask them what the difference is between the content of the first and second paragraph.

Give plenty of practice in writing well-sequenced paragraphs of about half to two-thirds of a page.

How long is a paragraph?

Emphasise to students that different types of writing require different lengths of paragraphs; for example, a newspaper report will have more, shorter paragraphs than an argumentative essay, and a letter will normally start and finish with short, one- or two-sentence paragraphs and have longer ones in the middle. Students also need to know about changing paragraphs when a different person speaks.

However, it is safer to start from the premise that a paragraph gathers up all the information that constitutes a section of a story, description or argument, and that you would expect most paragraphs to be at least half a page long. It is confusing for a reader to be confronted with three sides presented in twelve paragraphs, when it would be perfectly possible for parts of the content to be gathered together into larger sections. Time needs to be spent on this, emphasising the longer paragraph and then showing how different lengths of paragraph can be used for special effects, especially in fiction.

Overall structure

Before students can write, they need a **plan**, and there are many, many ways in which individuals like to plan. They might:

- write Para 1, Para 2, Para 3 etc. on a piece of paper and put under each of the headings some notes, a keyword or an opening sentence;
- draw a spider diagram so they can add some details to their main headings, and not decide on the actual order until they start to write – in the following diagram, a student has brainstormed six possible paragraph headings, each with three ideas, any of which might be developed within the paragraph;

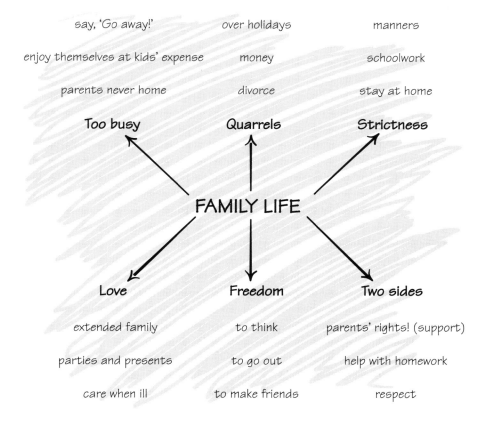

- draw a series of boxes and fill them with notes;
- draw thumbnail sketches to provide them with icons for each paragraph;
- plan in their heads.

The important thing is how their writing is to progress. Is the shape going to be introduction, points for, points against, personal preference and conclusion? If they argue a case for a controversial topic, do they save their strongest argument until last and build up to it? A good test for the order of an argument is to see whether the paragraphs could equally well have been put in another order; if so, there is generally a weakness in the plan.

Writing an argument
In the classroom, it is difficult to set topics that are not very traditional. How should a popular topic like the following one be planned and written in a fresh and interesting way? Compare two ways of starting.

Student activity 4.5	introductions – the advantages of a sporting life

Version 1 (beginning):

> Some years ago they experimented on French schoolchildren to discover whether those who did a whole day of academic work scored higher marks in examinations than those who practised sport every afternoon. Children who exercised were better academically. Lately, scientists have discovered that exercise and sunshine make your brain more active and your mood more positive. Since there should be balance in everything, you would expect a diet of science, the arts and sports to produce generally active and satisfied people. Not everybody can be a star performer or should follow a dedicated life of training, but some element of sport in one's life should benefit your outlook on life.

Version 2 (beginning):

> I lead a sporting life and think that it has lots of advantages. I am especially keen on football and play for my school team. We go all over Europe and to several schools in Africa, so we meet lots of people. I really enjoyed going to Alexandria where there were lots of sights to see. I think a sporting life guarantees your fitness as well. I have to train every day in the gym and I feel very fit. I think it is good because it makes you have a competitive spirit which is very useful these days.

Use these examples to discuss with your students which is the better opening, and why? Get them to suggest how each example might lead to the rest of the writing and which one – or both – might ultimately succeed.

Version 1 starts with two different ideas that may be new to some readers and attract their attention; this leads to a reasoned argument that sport appears to be good for everyone, but no attempt is made to bully the reader. The writer leaves plenty of space to develop the rest of the writing. In the second opening, the writer throws ideas at the reader in no particular order and, one suspects, has very little to say. The content is presented from a highly personal point of view, whereas the first example is far more objective. There are also problems of style in version 2.

Student activity 4.6	planning an essay – the advantages of a sporting life

Use version 1 from Student activity 4.5 as an opening and get the students to plan the rest of the essay so that the paragraphs are in a convincing order.

Here is a checklist of activities to advise students about how to use paragraphs effectively:
- practise writing well-sequenced paragraphs with topic sentences;
- start with paragraphs of a reasonable length and then show how and when that length should be varied;
- study ways of linking one paragraph to another;
- make plans of non-narrative writing that avoid repetition.

A sense of audience – writing in different registers

In First Language English, students are expected to adopt different registers according to different people, purposes and contexts. The language used will reflect various degrees of formality. A good way to approach this is through letters, which have the advantages of comparative brevity, an accepted structure and a great number of possible contexts and registers that can be used. As far as teaching is concerned, it is preferable to assume that an email should be written like a letter.

Student activity 4.7	introductory letter

Teacher: Someone you know slightly is moving to our area and is probably coming to our school. You decide to write a letter to give that person information about both the area and the school. Start by reintroducing yourself.

The short, introductory paragraph sets the tone of the letter, friendly but perhaps quite formal. The main part of the letter, being informative, needs to be clear and straightforward. Undue informality and jokey comments would blur the message. An appropriate introduction could be:

Dear Jacantha,

I hope you remember me. We met two years ago when I was on holiday in Harare, and some friends told me that you are coming to school here. I thought I'd write to you to give you some idea of what you are in for!

Student activity 4.8   letter of complaint

Teacher: Write a letter of complaint about something you bought that went wrong. Maybe you're tempted to write a very long letter, full of clever language. If you do, they'll only read it out to each other and laugh at you. So be well mannered and clear and exact about what has gone wrong. Be even clearer about what you want done about it. Use three paragraphs, the first giving an exact description of the article, and where and when you bought it. Then explain fully what has gone wrong. In the last paragraph, explain what action you want them to take. You could write similar letters about a bus that ran early and you missed it or a holiday that went wrong. Can you think of a real example from your own experience?

You could invent right and wrong ways to do this such as:

1

Dear Sir/Madam

Dana Computer, model w54/ur

I am writing to you about the problems I have had with this computer which I bought from Jenna electronics last month.

2 | Dear Sir/Madam

In all my life as an expert computer programmer working for many prestigious firms, I have never encountered so many problems with any electronic machinery as with your model w54/ur which I purchased recently from our local branch of the renowned Jenna electronics under the delusion that I would be the proud possessor of something upon which I could rely for many years to come.

3 | Dear Sir/Madam

Your firm is a disgrace. I have never seen such a load of complete rubbish as the plastic nonsense you are pleased to call a computer.
You ought to be ashamed of yourself.

You could start to invent words to describe different registers: (1) could be plain and straightforward; (2) could be verbose; and (3) could be insulting.

Student activity 4.9 **letter to parents**

Teacher: While we're on the subject of letters, what about a letter to parents from the Principal? You know the sort of thing: 'Dear Parent, I am writing to inform you of a new school rule I have had to enforce owing to ...' Let's think of some reasons why the Principal might write to all the parents or to your parents. Then choose one and write the letter. Write in the Principal's style and then discuss the sort of language you have used. Is it different from your own style? How? Why? Now try writing the same letter using a real teenage style and discuss the differences.

This is normally a good exercise to test the extremes of register, and you could turn the tables by getting students to write a typical letter to a best friend who has just left the school for another country, and then writing the same letter in the Principal's style.

Student activity 4.10 **explanatory letter**

Teacher: We could write lots of different letters. Here's a tricky one. You'd promised to do something on a particular day for a member of your family or a dear friend, but something more important has come up. You write a letter to explain yourself

(you are not staying with the person concerned at the time –
hence the letter). You'll have to make some decisions like what
the event or the promise was, who the person is and what the
'more important' happening was. However, you should know
that the person concerned has been known to take offence
quite easily. When you have finished, try the exercise again,
but this time make it a conversation and see what differences
of content and language it leads you into. You can read the
conversations out loud at the end.

This requires a register that will be appropriate for someone the writer
knows very well, but to whom, in this case, they must show real tact.

Teacher activity 4.2 (discussion)

Discuss the difficulties your students may encounter in writing in
different registers.
Discuss different registers that you might suggest for writing stories, for
example books for young children and different sorts of storytellers.
Discuss how you might teach techniques and persuasion as used by
media writers, and show how the use of emotive language might affect
different target groups.

Teaching the technical aspects of writing

The two most important areas to develop are:

- the breadth of vocabulary;
- the ability to construct sentences.

The most common sources of error are:

- punctuation, especially the correct use of full stops and commas;
- spelling;
- correct use of the verb, especially sequence of tenses;
- leaving out essential words;
- incorrect prepositions;
- inappropriately literal translations from the writer's first language
  to English.

How do you currently deliver this aspect of English? Have you been in schools that do it differently? Do you find that what you teach as a lesson is reflected in what students write, or are there problems of transferability?

Some of you will be in schools that deliver a structured language course. For example, if all your students are Spanish, you will be in the business of turning them into effective bilingual writers and speakers. A course like this is easy to organise and is likely to be effective. It is more difficult if you have classes of mixed nationalities and varied linguistic experience, or where a proportion of the students are already first-language users.

In these classes, some of your work will be tailored to individuals and some will be class-based. You have these options:

- Spend the first ten minutes of every lesson teaching or practising some aspect of linguistic competence. It might be a group of words that demonstrate a convention of spelling or it might be a simple exercise in which students put full stops into an unpunctuated paragraph and discuss what they have done. It is a way of starting a lesson promptly and it achieves something positive in very little time. You can also remind them of the start of the lesson as they leave the room at the end.
- Draw students' attention to a technical point as it occurs in the lesson. For example, they are preparing to write a story where they will need to include dialogue, and it is an appropriate moment to remind them of the punctuation they will need.
- Pause in the reading of a text to demonstrate a feature of the writer's style, for example the use of complex and simple sentences for effect. Turn complex sentences into simple sentences and ask students to say which they prefer and why.
- Annotate students' work clearly. Research shows that students appreciate a comment on the content, the technique and the presentation. In commenting on technique, a summary of the main points illustrated in your marginal comments is very helpful. Perhaps this can be followed up by personal discussion with a view to improvement in future.

Work with words – spelling and vocabulary

As students learn new words, they should also learn to spell them. Bad spellers were made long before you met them and every time they spelled a new word wrongly, they learned that spelling. Hence 'tommorow' and 'accomodation' are lodged in some people's memories for life. Notice how some people spell simple words incorrectly but can manage 'parallelogram' and 'rhombus' with ease. That suggests a changed attitude towards spelling, particularly of technical terms which they use commonly and where maths teachers make special efforts about the spelling. It's a long haul, but it's never too late to change an attitude towards spelling.

There are many different ways to improve spelling ability:

- To a large extent, your work is remedial. Invite students to face up to their spelling problems and promise them that with a real effort they can be largely cured in three years, as some studies claim. The time span will come as a shock, but your confidence will have an effect.
- It is a good idea to do something with spelling corrections. You could collect them from all the books in the class from a particular homework and set them as a test, or students could work in pairs, testing each other on their mistakes.
- To learn a spelling:
  – look at the word;
  – say the word;
  – cover it up;
  – write it from memory (don't just copy).
- Use notebooks to:
  – build up a vocabulary of daily words that you have found in the stories and poems you have read with them – invite students to use them in sentences of their own, or to make one of them part of the title of a story or poem of their own;
  – keep a record of all the spelling mistakes they make – get parents to test them at home and sign the book when they have done so.
- Find a suitable dictionary and thesaurus and make sure everyone in the class has a copy during the lesson. Teach dictionary skills, such as alphabetical order to the third letter and how to find a word you cannot spell. Try looking up all the words that begin with 'cata'. Run dictionary competitions, such as ten words to look up in ten minutes, or a game where four people give and defend definitions of a rare word, and the class must find who is right. When a student asks you for a spelling, give the first three letters and make them find the word. Teach about the origin of words and the fact that many words have more than one meaning, and why. Have a copy of a good etymological dictionary handy so that a student can see a complete entry and history of a word. Make sure that the thesaurus is comparatively simple. The traditional Roget is misleading for most people and has much that is outdated and even archaic. There are several school editions around, and you can try website thesauruses.

- Test spelling regularly. It is essential to remind students at all times that without words they cannot communicate, so constantly draw attention to words that may be new, and get them to use them, both in writing and in talk. Put a premium on using new words, and test their spelling.
- Draw attention to the sounds of words – soft-sounding words like 'pale', 'low', 'rustle' and hard, violent words like 'juggernaut', 'frazzle', 'trash can'. Learning technical terms can be a waste of time, but 'onomatopoeia' and 'alliteration' work because they are easy to understand and to explain in terms of the effects that words make. Before an assignment invite the students themselves to draw up a list of words that they can use. Then you may add additional words.
- You can encourage wordgames and crosswords for those who like them. Show Latin origins by writing words like 'tract' and getting the class to supply prefixes (ex-, sub-, at-, con-, etc.) and suffixes (-ed, -ion, -ing, -ive) as a diagram and then a list of all the possible words. This helps spelling and vocabulary.

Every lesson should contain something about working with words, which will eventually enhance the quality of the writing of your classes.

Teacher activity 4.4 (planning)

Think of next week's work with any class you teach. In what ways can you include work with words in each of your lessons? What sort of approach to working with words will be appropriate with different age groups?

Are you satisfied with the spelling ability of your students, or do you need to add anything to the way you manage it?

Sentences and full stops

Writing well-formed sentences is one of the most important indications that students are expressing themselves coherently. How often have you found something like this?

> Alma was a little old lady, all the neighbours loved her. She loved flowers, she had a garden full of them, they looked beautiful all the year round.

Five simple sentences, nearly all of which are incorrectly punctuated, since pronouns (she, they) are not connectives and do not join sentences together. But the crime of bad punctuation is compounded by the equally bad crime of using only simple sentences that do not read fluently and do not show relationships between ideas.

This would be better:

> Meet Alma, a little old lady who is loved by all her neighbours. She has a garden full of lovely flowers which look beautiful all the year round.

It doesn't take much effort to produce this (indeed, the first example may be a product of laziness rather than ignorance), although it does require knowledge of how a sentence may become a phrase and the use of 'who' and 'which'.

Commas

With the advent of word processing, students use commas more rarely and with less accuracy. There is little awareness that they affect precise meaning:

- Commas should be used to cut off a subordinate clause from a main clause when the subordinate clause starts the sentence (e.g. 'If you haven't got tickets for the gig in advance, then you might as well not bother going'). If both clauses are very short, then the comma is often left out (e.g. 'If you're unwell consult your doctor').
- Students must be careful to look at where a phrase begins *and* ends if they wish to insert commas (e.g. 'A terror campaign cannot succeed unless we become its accomplices and, out of fear, give in'), where a common mistake would be to omit the comma before 'out'.

Using grammar

It is a good idea to work with parts of speech, gradually developing more complex sentences:

- Start with **nouns**.
- Do **verbs** next, because then you can show what a **sentence** is. Tenses come later.
- Move on to **connectives, starting with conjunctions**. Make a list of not more than 20 (e.g. and, but, or, so, because, for, since, although, who, which, that, when, after, where, before, until, if). Discourage the use of 'then', all pronouns and 'this' when joining sentences, as these words are not connectives.

Try joining these sentences together:

- I sang. She burst into tears.

What is meant by:

- When I sang, she burst into tears.
- She burst into tears, although I sang.
- I sang because she burst into tears.
- She burst into tears because I sang.

In other words, when you use one of these words to join sentences, it defines meaning.

You are now in a position to start to show how sentences can be built up.

- Add **adjectives** and show the difference in detail between a sentence with adjectives and one without. Show how adjectives add to clarity of meaning.
- Then add **adverbs** as above. Younger students can act out different types of walking, talking, looking, or other types of behaviour when you say the adverb.
- Lastly, teach **prepositions** and, therefore, phrases, but don't bother with their being noun, adjectival or adverbial phrases – just show how phrases can be used in building up sentences.

Give practice in turning lists of simple sentences into complex sentences.

Using short sentences for effect

Students need to be careful not to write overlong, shapeless sentences which blur meaning. In their writing they should be able to learn to use short sentences for effect, as in the following example where the two short sentences imitate the action and the immediate thoughts of the main character in the story.

> Endean stuffed his hands in his overcoat pockets for protection against the cold wind and hurried along the dark passageway, concerned about the reception he was about to get from a wife still angry from the disagreement they had had earlier that day. Suddenly he stopped. What was that noise? He heard it again, an odd, snarling noise which seemed to come from the bushes that lay ominously, just in front of him, on his left and could, Endean realised, harbour all sorts of frightening and angry creatures.

Further examples of the patterns of sentence construction that writers use can be found in the texts that you study on a daily basis.

Tenses

There are two problems, one a first-language and the other a second-language difficulty.

First-language students often start their work in a present tense and drift into a past tense. Sometimes they subsequently drift back and forth. Solve the problem by making them read their work over again. Second-language students often confuse present, future and conditional tenses.

These students also need instruction in the right use of the preposition and in problems of literal translation. Common errors are, 'I am in London since three weeks' and the wrong use of the plural 'advices' and the word 'desesperated'.

LOOKING BACK

In your lessons, how can you make your students aware of the importance of:

◆ using their senses, their memories and their research to find and develop content;

◆ sequencing individual paragraphs and structuring a piece of writing so that it is in the best order and has internal balance;

◆ developing vocabulary to attract the reader's interest and to provide clarity;

◆ developing fluency by learning to create well-ordered sentences in which the links between ideas are clearly shown;

◆ understanding the appropriate register to use for different audiences in different contexts;

◆ understanding the use of correct punctuation and grammar and learning to spell?

How can you create an atmosphere where all students are aware of their progress as writers during all their time in the school?

5 Setting up coursework

Some examinations include coursework or give you the option of coursework instead of components which would otherwise be examined externally.

Coursework is a collection of pieces of writing completed over a period of time, usually internally assessed (by you, the teacher) and externally moderated (by your examining board). Precise requirements of coursework differ between syllabus specifications, but usually require completion of a portfolio of different types of writing by the student.

In any case, the particular features of coursework are that no time is specified as to how long may be spent on a piece of work, the assignments may be negotiated within the school and the students take responsibility for developing and presenting their work.

The main advantages of coursework are that the written responses:
- dovetail with your own schemes of work and do not dominate teaching;
- map the progress of the student's developing skills;
- are a selection of the best of which the student is capable.

Choosing assignments

Coursework gives you extra responsibility for setting up the work, for advising candidates how to improve it and for marking it. You will spend time discussing the process with your colleagues and, although this will take time, it will increase your professionalism and your skills in task setting and assessment. For example, there are differences between taking an examination paper and setting up a coursework task.

Scenario 1

Maria is discussing task setting with her colleague, Vicki.

Maria: Vicki, George came up to me this morning. He reckoned he'd got coursework sorted out. 'Easy,' he said. 'What I'm going to do is to set them three or four topics from last year's examination paper. They can do them in exam conditions, so I don't have to prepare lessons, and I can catch up with my marking while they are writing.

Vicki: I don't see that there is any advantage in that. They might as
(looking well do the exam.
puzzled)

Vicki is right. George is missing many good educational opportunities and reducing the validity of the coursework. By setting an old examination paper, he has failed to connect the assignment either to the development of the student as writer or to his teaching programme. There's no opportunity for drafting and redrafting – he may save himself time and trouble, but he is not teaching his students self-assessment or letting them criticise each other's work.

Let's look at a different way in which George might work.

Teacher activity 5.1 (planning)

Suppose a major issue has sprung up locally; maybe a world famous band cannot perform because its music is regarded as overtly rebellious or offensive in some other way, or there is a scandal affecting the performance of your city's football team. You decide to take up one of these issues and study the opposing arguments made in various newspapers and other media, and then examine the moral and social issues. As in previous examples, you cover important aspects of reading and speaking and listening and practise important thinking skills. All this leads to a writing task which might be:

Is honesty and integrity important in public institutions? How do you react to the scandal concerning the football club and what do you think ought to happen? How does all this relate to life in general?

The first thing you notice is that the task is longer than a topic normally set in an examination paper, because you want students to be specific about the one incident, but also broaden the issue to explore other aspects of life. Similarly, a literature topic would reflect those aspects of a text, some more difficult than others, that you wished to cover in relation to your teaching.

Here are some topics taken at random from folders from different parts of the world:

> Cultivation in Brazil, What did you have for dinner?, The Olympics, Be prepared, Television is a drug, Technology and the new millennium, Examinations are a necessary evil, Why have guns?, Football in the Cayman Islands, Music censorship, A brochure for the dance society, Teenage pregnancy, Taking risks is better than leading a dull life, Dragons.

Teacher activity 5.2 (discussion)

Which of these topics are unlike those set in examination papers and why? What sort of preparation might these teachers' students have done before writing about them?

Strategies for planning and setting up appropriate coursework tasks

Scenario 2

George has had second thoughts and has become so enthusiastic about linking coursework to the curriculum, that Maria and Vicki have started to avoid him. However, he catches Maria during coffee break.

George: What are you doing for your first assignment, Maria?

Maria: I found a couple of good articles, one about women's rights in Africa and the other about women in the home. We could read them together and I'd set a title, something like 'Women's rights in the twenty-first century', and they'd all do that for their argument.

George: Um, very good, but wouldn't they all use the same ideas? I can see them lifting wholesale from your two articles – they sound too good not to be copied.

Maria: All right, George, what have you decided to do, now you are
(sarcasti- converted to real education?
cally)

George: I thought I'd look at it differently. I'd help them to understand the
(paying skills of building up arguments and then the sorts of language you
no could use. There are lots of skills involved in selecting language
attention) here. We'd look at one or two speeches, you know, 'I have a dream' and so on, and then various forms of getting ideas across in writing – a newspaper article and a website perhaps; I think the Body Shop

website goes into issues – oh, and there are some spoof speeches in 'Animal Farm' which they've just finished reading. We'll try a few outrageous ones of our own, and when we've got the idea, I'll ask them what topics really make them stirred up inside. It'll take a bit of time, but I guarantee they'll enjoy it and the writing will be original.

Maria: That's really good, George. I might just try it myself.

Maria – a good idea, but it needs thinking through

Maria has a good topic which will energise both girls and boys, but George is right, the better the articles, the more they will form the basis of the students' work. Another problem is that the title is vague. Something about traditional roles and change, or a chance to write about marriage might narrow down the topic and give individuals more chance to show what they can do. Maria could also ask her students to suggest their own titles and forms of writing arising from her introduction to the topic.

George – his method will make his students think

Maria's work is good, but George seems to be nearer the heart of the matter. He is teaching skills and technique, for example the planning of an argument so that there is progression, not repetition; how to use language that will persuade people; how to link paragraphs appropriately. He is using good, varied stimuli (campaigning speech, media/website and literature) to interest his students and to give them experience of high-quality speakers and writers. Reading, writing and speaking and listening will integrate well in these lessons. He will also kick-start students' thinking skills because they will really respond to the stimuli he proposes and there will be little likelihood of copying.

Practising subskills relating to the writing of short stories

You can use the same sort of approach towards other sorts of tasks. You might choose a few stories (perhaps a book of short stories set for a literature examination) – or start with a folk story or a children's story and analyse the ways they gain the readers' attention. Your students would experience ways of beginning and plot the sort of information the writer provides, the way that the story builds up to its main point, whether that be frightening, adventurous or comic, and what happens at the end. They would encounter flashbacks, time lapses and little lines of stars. Students could learn how to use the briefest of hints about characterisation and settings. They would understand how tension is built up and atmosphere provided. They might also study some of the features of a genre such as a ghost or horror story. Through these experiences they would learn the subskills that are necessary for those who wish to practise the very enjoyable habit of writing short stories.

You would then apply what had been learnt to writing a short story for coursework. Students would choose their own title and you would be available to discuss ways of including some of the devices common to fiction, and thus reinforce what you had taught.

Analysing and practising subskills associated with media studies

If you do not already include media studies as an important part of your teaching, you should consider the importance of media in your students' world. Teach them to be critical of what they read, hear and see. Impress upon them that the stimuli are up to date and take less time to study than works of literature, but that the skills that they need to handle them are wide ranging and very similar to those required for literature.

As examples of what you can do, you will be busy demonstrating the methods by which advertisers catch their prey through graphics, colour, words and the moving image. Your classes will be dissecting the language of travel brochures, and comparing stories in competing newspapers, and detecting their political allegiance. You may start a course in film or photographic studies. Your students will create excellent media texts of their own and write detailed and powerful analyses of texts they have studied.

Teacher activity 5.3 (discussion)

Discuss ways in which media studies can be integrated into English work over a period of years, or how you might plan a term's work to use all the available English time. What English objectives would you be likely to cover (especially the thinking skills) and how would this work relate to your students' general progress in English?

Drafting and redrafting

You could argue that drafting and redrafting is an essential part of the writing process, but it is of great significance in coursework, and some examination boards ask for first drafts as well as the final versions of pieces of work.

It is important not to throw oneself into writing – as many students do. Reflection and/or discussion before writing saves problems later. But equally an assignment should not last for ever. There are other things to do, and one piece of writing is only a stage in someone's personal development as a writer. It is wise when talking to students, to expect improvement from assignment to assignment through practice and maturing.

Students preparing coursework should, for each piece, show you:
- a plan (which we have already dealt with in Chapter 4);
- a first draft;
- a final version.

The first draft should be as careful and as neat as possible; obviously there are great advantages in word processing since there will be no ugly crossings out, sections can easily be moved from one place to another, and rewording is a normal, not an onerous business. Students who word process the plan, the first draft and the final version should provide you with printed copies of each stage and should be encouraged to explain what they have done.

The first draft gives opportunities for discussion. The outcomes are:
- revising;
- editing;
- correcting.

Your students will often believe that the last of these and cleaning up the text are the only reasons for redrafting. However, revising and editing are more important and need teaching. You may hope for a reasonably correct first draft anyway.

Revising, editing and correcting can be a paired activity in which students make helpful suggestions about one another's work.

Revising

Here are two examples of what is meant by revision. In the first, the teacher persuades a student to achieve a better balance in his writing by shortening it, and in the second, the ending to a story is redrafted.

Scenario 3

Teacher: Kuldip, I think you put a superb effort into this story about moving house. Seven sides is a lot. The start was great. Your first line, 'I had spent all my young life in this house' and then a few of the details that really meant something to you – that really made me feel I was a part of the story. Then you explained why you had to move and brought me up to date. The third section was where you described how they brought out the furniture and put it in the truck. Now that section went on for two and a half sides, and you lost me there. I think you should cut that down to about half a side.

Kuldip: But it took me hours to write this story.

Teacher: I know, and you did well, but we can make the story better. We need to get to your new house and your feelings about moving into something strange.

Kuldip: Well, I don't know.

Teacher: Perhaps you describe too many items of furniture.

Kuldip: Perhaps I could just write about three that really meant something to me and I couldn't imagine what they would look like in the new house. And then I could add something about something that Mum and Dad didn't take and I was surprised.

Teacher: That would be great. I think I would be really interested to *(smiling* read that.
triumphantly)

It's a set-up, but Kuldip, not the teacher, did the work and kept ownership of the writing.

Scenario 4

Teacher: Your science fiction story was good, most ingenious about how all the destruction came about and they had to hide in the underground cavern. But I thought the ending was disappointing.

Athene: How would you have done it then?

Teacher: Ah, well, umm, perhaps I'd have finished with some hint of hope for the future when your main character opens the hatch and ventures out into the old world.

Athene: No, I don't think that fits into the earlier part. I'll tell you what I'll do ...

If she had accepted the teacher's suggestion, it probably wouldn't have worked. As it is, Athene retains ownership.

In both examples, revising involves substantial changes to a first draft. Other examples could be:

- adding descriptive passages or developing and explaining arguments in pieces of writing which have little content or do not give enough detail to interest a reader;
- changing prosaic beginnings to ones that would attract attention (e.g. the story about Greta in Chapter 4);
- changing the order of sections or paragraphs.

Revisions should be made in response to your advice or the question, 'Are you satisfied with the content and order of this writing?' asked by you.

Editing

This is about changes made to individual words, phrases and sentences because:

- their meaning is not clear;
- they do not make the necessary impact;
- it takes too long to make a simple point;
- the register is wrong.

You would encourage students to edit by making comments like these:

'I really thought that the language you used was wrong. You were describing a relatively simple set of events in very long words, and I'm not sure you knew what all of them meant.'

'Why do you always use two words where one would do? Let's look at one or two grammatical devices that would save you all these words.'

'Now this is a place where you would benefit by using one or two adjectives to make your descriptions more vivid.'

Correcting

There are three levels of correcting:

- You do the correcting and the student amends the first draft. You hope that copying will teach the correct spelling, punctuation or grammar. *This is not allowed if the piece is to be used for a coursework in an examination*.
- You indicate each error by S or P, for example, and the student has to find the correct version.
- You give a general comment or advice, and the student has to find where the errors are and make the correction. *This is the preferred method for coursework examinations.*

The first method is likely to be used with younger students and with those who are not really first-language users. The other methods are used with students who are more conversant with English conventions and have a more extensive vocabulary.

Proofreading is not a popular pastime! However, it is important since a large number of errors occur through carelessness. In word processing the number of mistakes is frequently greater than in handwritten scripts because of typing errors, unthinking use of the spellchecker, and inability to make judgements when using the thesaurus. The less secure the student's language, the more likely are the errors when the spellchecker and the thesaurus show unfamiliar words. Students also forget that a proper English word may still be a misspelling. The spellchecker will not pick up 'form' when you meant 'from'.

LOOKING BACK

- ◆ Does coursework strike you as an educationally advantageous alternative to part of an examination assessment?
- ◆ To what extent do you think that coursework gives you more to do, or does it reflect what you ought to be doing anyway? Does coursework increase professionalism?
- ◆ What possibilities does a policy of revising, editing and correcting throughout the school offer to you and to your students?

6 A note on assessment

Teachers annotate students' work by indicating strengths and weaknesses in the text and by making comments. This example shows the dangers that can arise from evaluations that are not related to descriptions of performance derived from skills and objectives.

Scenario 1

Mercedes' teacher has written 'good' at the end of her story and has given a mark of 14 out of 20.

Mercedes: How good is 14? Will it get me a good grade in the exam?

Teacher: Oh yes, Mercedes. I really enjoyed your story. It reminded me of my grandmother when I was your age.

Mercedes: Is my English good enough?

Teacher: Yes, I could understand almost all of your story.

What does 'good' mean here? Is it in comparison with others in the class, or a subjective response? Does Mercedes or the teacher know the criteria to which 'good' relates? What sort of 'good' grade is it? After all, only fourteen marks have been given. Finally, the teacher's comment about being able to read 'almost all of your story' suggests there are linguistic difficulties that would preclude Mercedes from achieving a high grade. It's all very misleading.

In the next example, the teacher comments on how the work demonstrates Mercedes' grasp of the various skills of writing.

Scenario 2

This time the teacher has written: 'Your story is very well managed and structurally clever. Your range of vocabulary is wide, and your choice of detail vivid. The work is fluent and easy to read in places. Your spelling is rather careless, and you are still joining sentences with commas. Your story is neatly written. 15 marks.'

Mercedes: When you gave a mark of 15, how much did you take off for my spelling and full stops?

Teacher: I thought the story was so good that it deserved 18, in the top band. I took 3 marks off for the errors, which would give it a lower grade.

Mercedes: OK. I know how to write a story, but the next stage is to improve my punctuation and spelling.

This time there is no doubt in Mercedes' mind about the level she has reached or what she has to do next.

Writing descriptions of performance

If you and your colleagues all follow the same marking criteria and students are aware of them, there will be no confusion, as there was in Scenario 1.

You can assess anything you want. Let's take a simple example of cross-country running. A simple criterion is to reach a point within a set time. You decide on three levels of performance:

A Runs powerfully and arrives before the set time
B Runs consistently and arrives within the set time limits
C Runs hesitantly and arrives outside the set time

As the runners arrive they are given A, B or C and you can now comment on their standard, particularly if they run similarly on subsequent occasions.

The more criteria you want to include, the more complex the task is. Suppose you want to write descriptions for reading aloud in English. The descriptions will be for five mark bands as follows:

A Excellent
B Good
C Average
D Less good
E Just acceptable

You decide on these criteria: accuracy, fluency, reading with emphasis and feeling. Now you write your descriptions and translate 'excellent', 'average' and 'just acceptable' into something more meaningful:

A Recognises all words confidently and reads even complex sentences with fluency and at an appropriate speed; emphasises keywords to communicate shades of meaning, and responds to tone, especially in dialogue.

C Reads most words accurately and is generally fluent with only occasional hesitancy. Adapts voice to the style of the piece and emphasises some words to communicate meaning.

E Despite frequent mistakes and hesitancy over words, the listener can make out the overall meaning. Some individual sentences may be read fluently. The voice is without expression for the most part.

Teacher activity 6.1 (writing)

Your task is to write the descriptions for bands B and D. You will find it awkward to make your descriptions look different from the two adjacent ones, and it is a nuisance to have to cope with three different criteria for each description. You may use the word 'some', but try to avoid it as much as possible. Descriptions of performance are normally written in the present tense.

It is difficult not to make your descriptions too wordy. They can be reduced to note form, in various sorts of grids, and they are best when they include easily memorised phrases. However, that goes well beyond the scope of this short chapter.

How to use descriptions of performance

If you have descriptions for different types of English activity, all composed by (a) selecting the criteria; and (b) developing those criteria as shown above, you can all work to one standard.

Use this procedure:

- Find the description that is the best fit, that most nearly matches the work for assessment.
- If it fits exactly, award the top mark in the band, but check the higher description in case it is a better fit.
- If it fits most of the description, award a lower mark in the band, but check the lower description in case it is a better fit.
- In any case, always consider two adjacent descriptions.

Next time you come across a similar marking scheme published by an examining board, you will know how it has been constructed and how to use it. Remember that you can make up your own descriptions of performance for any skill-based activity for students of all ages.

Conclusion

With assessment, the wheel comes full circle. We started by considering the pattern of skills we should build into our lessons, explored how those skills could be developed so that each student would make measurable progress as a speaker, listener, reader and writer, and finally gained a little insight into how we could make reliable comments about standards of performance.

We are at the dawn of an electronics revolution and can already access information which was almost totally unavailable to us just a few years ago. Word processing allows us to revise and edit our work so easily that our notions of composition have already changed. Gradually more and more people will have access to this sort of machinery.

However, we have already seen that the new age is making considerable extra demands on our reading and writing skills, and this process is likely to increase over the next few years as technology advances. What if it became normal to write by speaking into a machine which then printed what we had just said? Think how the focus would shift onto our ability to revise and edit. How would we have to refocus our teaching if we were implanted with chips that could communicate our thoughts?

It is a brave new world, and it is through highly developed communication skills that we shall be empowered to meet it.

Appendix A: Resources

What you use for teaching depends on your philosophy and how much time you can spend creating your own materials. If you use a coursebook the work is done for you, but the ideas are someone else's; if you teach largely from literature, you can choose activities that reflect your own interests, but you also have to amass a collection of non-literary texts. Remember that a stimulus for an assignment does not have to be long, and that photographs count as texts.

Coursebooks   Changes in the examination specifications in England have resulted in new series of textbooks, including shorter books on specific aspects of learning, such as grammar. Many books that explore media are available. New books serving examinations specifically offered outside England have also recently been published. Exam boards often issue their own suggested resources lists which are worth consulting. The publishers' websites vary in ease of navigation, but offer much excellent information, including sample pages from some of the books.

Literature   Most skills can be taught through fiction, drama and poetry without using coursebooks. However, you need a large stock to prevent having to use titles that are not popular in the class.

Newspapers and magazines   You can access a great number of newspapers online. Some websites such as www.guardian.co.uk have an archive. There are several websites that give access to newspapers worldwide or which republish articles. An example is http://allafrica.com. An interesting website that needs a little patience when sorting through the results of its searches is www.findarticles.com. National Geographic has a very popular website, and you can buy CD-ROMs of articles from publications like *National Geographic* and *Time* magazine.

Websites   These are potentially your best non-literary resources, although you need patience and skill in giving your search engine the right instructions. Working out which extra word will produce exactly what you want is a skill in itself. Students should be encouraged to research for themselves, and you can give them printouts for comparison and for practice in using their own words.

Radio and the moving image   Plenty of good, analytical work arises from the use of TV and film studies. World radio is available via the

Internet. You can study techniques used in all sorts of programmes and create some of them by yourself.

Advertisements and commercials   These are excellent for analysis and for the study of language. Teach students to create their own advertisements and advertising campaigns.

People   If you can, bring in visitors to talk and to be interviewed. You can hire poets and travelling drama groups. You can invite local medical workers, police, dignitaries, employers, older people with their memories and people with unusual jobs. Students learn to ask questions, chair discussions, make notes and write articles. Perhaps you could have a media day with reporters from the local newspaper and newscasters from the radio and TV station working with students.

Appendix B: Glossary

aim	long-term target
assessment	identifying a standard reached by a student
assignment	task (usually researched, planned, drafted and redrafted)
audience	specified reader or listener
context	situation to which writing or speaking is suited
criterion	principle on which someone can be judged
curriculum	all that has to be taught
departmental policy	agreed procedures followed by all subject teachers
directed writing	where instructions are given as to the content
emotive language	words intended to evoke associations and feelings (mostly in media texts)
gist	main ideas without detail
mark bands	marks allocated for each division in a mark scheme
media	the mass communication organisations
monitor	check progress
objective	short-term target
outcome	what happens as a result of what you teach
process talk	discussion that helps to complete an assignment
reading records	lists of what has been read, kept by the student
register	choice of language suitable to audience and context
scanning	looking for references in texts
search engine	website that finds other websites to your command
self-assessment	judgement of performance made by the student
skimming	quick reading for gist
specification	syllabus
standard English	English free of regional or social variants
strategy	plan of action
target audience/group	particular social or age group for whom a media text is intended
text	any written or visual document
transferability	the putting to general use by the student of something you have taught

Index